London 2012 Paralympic Games
The Official Book

First published by Carlton Books Limited
in 2012

Copyright © 2012 Carlton Books Limited

Carlton Books Limited
20 Mortimer Street
London, W1T 3JW

London 2012 emblems © The London
Organising Committee of the Olympic Games
and Paralympic Games Ltd (LOCOG) 2007.
London 2012 mascots ™ & ® LOCOG 2009-
2010. London 2012 pictograms © LOCOG
2009. All Rights Reserved.

A CIP catalogue record for this book is
available from the British Library.

10 9 8 7 6 5 4 3 2 1

Senior Editor: Conor Kilgallon
Design Direction: Darren Jordan and Luke Griffin
Production: Maria Petalidou
Written by: Press Association Sport

ISBN: 978-1-84732-922-6

FSC
MIX
Paper
FSC® C101537

Printed in China

All statistics are correct at
1 November 2011.

ABOVE: Fireworks light up the night sky as the Closing Ceremony of the Beijing 2008 Paralympic Games prepares the world for London 2012.

London 2012 Paralympic Games
The Official Book

Games schedule • Venues guide • Full event previews • Star athlete profiles

CARLTON

Contents

Foreword
Sebastian Coe KBE

The Paralympic Games is a unique event. From its beginnings on the lawns of Stoke Mandeville Hospital in 1948 to the massive multi-event spectacle it is today, the Games is one of the greatest sporting events on earth.

The scale of the Paralympic Games is now immense. More than 4,000 of the world's best disabled athletes from over 140 nations will make London 2012 the biggest and best Games yet, providing 12 days of unique sporting drama.

The Paralympic Games features elite athletes with a disability competing in over 500 medal events, with the emphasis placed on elite performance, irrespective of disability. Drama and sporting ability stand alongside a spirit of togetherness and achievement neatly summed up by the Games motto: 'Spirit in Motion'.

Paralympic events such as Athletics, Cycling and Swimming will be already familiar but some, such as Boccia, are less well-known, providing the Games with its own unique flavour. All 20 Paralympic sports are covered in this book, making it a unique guide to the festival of sport that will unfold from late August onwards. And for London 2012 new arenas, such as the Olympic Stadium and the Velodrome, will provide a stunning backdrop, along with iconic locations that already have famous histories, such as Greenwich Park and The Mall.

But it is the Paralympians who are the real focus of attention. Some of the athletes in this book are already well known. Oscar Pistorius, the 'Blade Runner', and Ellie Simmonds, a double gold medallist at the age of only 13, are just two. But there will be many more whose names will come to the fore by 9 September, when the Games come to a close.

Rio will host the next Games, in 2016. By then, London will have added its own signature to the history of these great Games.

Introduction

When the Paralympic Cauldron is lit on 29 August the London 2012 Paralympic Games will finally begin, marking the start of what promises to be a spectacular celebration of the very best disability sport.

The Games will see over 4,000 athletes from right across the globe taking part in 20 different sports over 11 days of competition in one of the most famous cities in the world.

To help you fully enjoy everything the event has to offer, *London 2012 Paralympic Games: The Official Book* is packed full of stats, facts, information and pictures covering every aspect of the Games.

Each sport, discipline and event is covered in great detail – from the tense tactical battles that will take place in Goalball, where the crowd watch on in absolute silence, to the fast and frenetic action in Wheelchair Fencing, every single one is explained here. You will also discover the rules and regulations of each sport and the history of how and when they came to take their place in the Paralympic Games.

In each sport, a classification system exists so that athletes from a wide variety of disability groups can compete against each other. Look out for fact boxes throughout the book that explain in detail each disability category and how athletes are classified according to their level of impairment.

Ever since the inaugural Paralympic Games were held in Rome in 1960, a host of major cities across the world have provided the platform for thousands of talented athletes to leave their mark. Paralympic Games legends such as Trischa Zorn, Chantal Petitclerc and Tanni Grey-Thompson are deserving of their place in sporting history having claimed medal after medal, and their impact is rightly honoured within this publication, along with a comprehensive list of records from Games gone by.

This year, several more star names will be trying to match those achievements – whether it is Wheelchair Tennis player Esther Vergeer, 'Blade Runner' Oscar Pistorius, teenage Swimming sensation Ellie Simmonds or Swedish shooter Jonas Jacobsson – and this book covers the leading athletes you should look out for during London 2012.

The full list of every single session that will take place at the Games is covered in a comprehensive at-a-glance schedule, with the dates of each sport listed along with details of each session, so that you will know exactly what to watch and when.

We will also tell you exactly where the action is due to take

David Beckham and Sir Steve Redgrave, part of the bid team, celebrate the announcement.

ABOVE: Crowds celebrate in Trafalgar Square in 2005 as London is awarded the Games.

RIGHT: Sebastian Coe with IOC Chairman Jacques Rogge at the bid announcement in Singapore seven years ago.

place with an extensive guide to the various venues.

London is ready to stage a Paralympic Games to be proud of, combining the very best of what is great about the tradition and history of the city and the Games itself with a sense of cutting edge and creativity that will give the event its own unique twist. Picture, for example, the sight of arrows being fired off in the Archery competition at The Royal Artillery Barracks, with its long and proud military history, or the Marathon competitors making their way to the finishing line on one of London's most famous stretches of road, The Mall. Add to that the spectacle of the brand new Olympic Stadium, which will form the centrepiece of the action.

You will discover all you need to know about these magnificent settings, both old and new, in a comprehensive overview to the venues of London 2012 – including distinctive construction features and the sports taking place at each facility, as well as where they are located and travel information to help spectators get there.

Sport is an ever-changing environment, meaning that all the competitors highlighted in this book will be hoping that injury or circumstance does not combine to prevent them from taking their place at the heart of the action when the curtain is raised on 29 August.

For all the athletes who take part in the showpiece, it will almost certainly represent the very pinnacle of their careers and an event the likes of which we have rarely seen before.

Hopefully you will have great fun reading this celebration of the London 2012 Paralympic Games.

Welcome to London 2012

London is ready to welcome the 2012 Paralympic Games. This year, the world's best disabled athletes will gather together in the English capital to showcase their talents and go for glory, watched by what are expected to be capacity crowds. From the glistening new Olympic Stadium to historic venues such as The Royal Artillery Barracks and Greenwich Park, the stage is set for what promises to be the biggest and the best Paralympic Games ever seen.

David Weir, defending champion in the men's 800m – T54, celebrates his gold medal at Beijing 2008.

Welcome to the Games

The best disabled athletes will come to London this year for 11 days of exciting and intense competition, as one of the most prestigious sporting spectacles, the Paralympic Games, arrives in one of the world's most famous cities.

After many years of planning and much preparation, the showpiece will finally arrive in London in August for the 14th staging of an event that has developed from humble beginnings into a truly global celebration of disability sport.

In many ways, there is no better place to play host than London – with this year's Games due to be staged not far from where Sir Ludwig Guttman helped to sow the first seeds of the Paralympic Movement when he devised a competition to help aid the rehabilitation of disabled war veterans at Stoke Mandeville Hospital in the 1940s.

From those very early days, the Games have offered hope and inspiration to thousands of athletes, as well as millions of other disabled people around the world, and the signs are that London 2012 will be no different.

Since winning the bid to stage the Games back in 2005, the city has thought big, and when the action begins, there will be a total of 284 sessions taking place across 20 different sports, with more than 2,100 medals set to be handed out.

So just what kind of Games can we expect? Well, as the event has grown over the years, so has the level of competition – and the millions of spectators who gather at one of 15 different competition venues can expect to see all that is great about disability sport at the very highest level.

British fans will create their own unique, partisan atmosphere and there will, of course, be strong home support for the likes of swimmer Ellie Simmonds, who captured two golds at the tender age of 13 in Beijing four years ago, and cyclist Darren Kenny, of whom big things are expected on the track at the impressive new 6,000-capacity Velodrome.

But the Games is now a worldwide spectacle, and just as much attention is likely to be focused on those such as American Swimming sensation Jessica Long – who has already

IPC President Sir Philip Craven.

amassed an amazing collection of nine Paralympic Games medals at the age of just 20 – or Swedish shooter Jonas Jacobsson – one of the world's most decorated male Paralympians – and, of course, the instantly-recognisable South African, known as the 'Blade Runner', Oscar Pistorius.

All those names will be among the star athletes vying for the headlines following the Opening Ceremony on 29 August, but right across the sports there will be hundreds, if not thousands, of similar captivating human stories – with each athlete able to tell of their own intriguing journey to London 2012.

Excitement has been building steadily for some time. For example, in September 2011 an International Paralympic Day was held in Trafalgar Square in London to celebrate and promote the Games, generating huge public interest. Likewise, the unveiling of the official Paralympic Games mascot was met with much fanfare, and Mandeville – who appropriately gets his name from the hospital at Stoke Mandeville where the Paralympic Movement started to take shape – is likely to become a familiar sight for spectators watching on their television sets right around the world.

London 2012 has also raised the bar in terms of generating

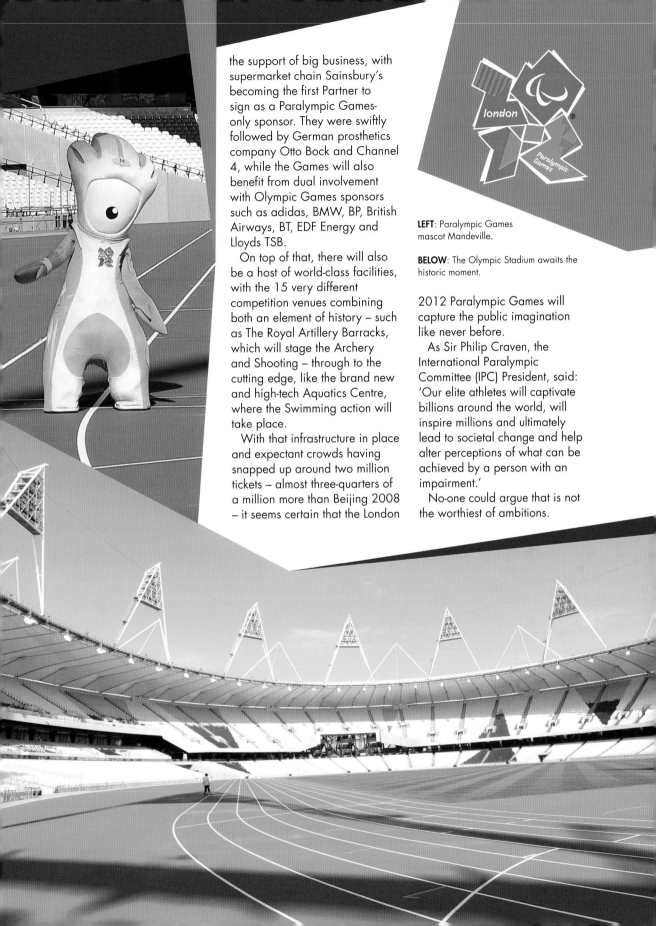

the support of big business, with supermarket chain Sainsbury's becoming the first Partner to sign as a Paralympic Games-only sponsor. They were swiftly followed by German prosthetics company Otto Bock and Channel 4, while the Games will also benefit from dual involvement with Olympic Games sponsors such as adidas, BMW, BP, British Airways, BT, EDF Energy and Lloyds TSB.

On top of that, there will also be a host of world-class facilities, with the 15 very different competition venues combining both an element of history – such as The Royal Artillery Barracks, which will stage the Archery and Shooting – through to the cutting edge, like the brand new and high-tech Aquatics Centre, where the Swimming action will take place.

With that infrastructure in place and expectant crowds having snapped up around two million tickets – almost three-quarters of a million more than Beijing 2008 – it seems certain that the London

LEFT: Paralympic Games mascot Mandeville.

BELOW: The Olympic Stadium awaits the historic moment.

2012 Paralympic Games will capture the public imagination like never before.

As Sir Philip Craven, the International Paralympic Committee (IPC) President, said: 'Our elite athletes will captivate billions around the world, will inspire millions and ultimately lead to societal change and help alter perceptions of what can be achieved by a person with an impairment.'

No-one could argue that is not the worthiest of ambitions.

History of the Games

The first official Paralympic Games were held in the 'Eternal City' of Rome in 1960 but it was back in 1948 at Stoke Mandeville Hospital in Aylesbury, England where the idea for the Paralympic Movement was first conceived.

Sir Ludwig Guttman, a neurologist at Stoke Mandeville, believed that sport had a key role to play in rehabilitating World War II veterans with spinal injuries. With that in mind, the German-born doctor organised a competition with other hospitals to coincide with the London 1948 Olympic Games. The event was named the International Wheelchair Games and took place on the same day that London 1948 started. Just 16 British war veterans competed and Archery was the only sport on the programme at the Buckinghamshire hospital. The competition was widely considered to be a roaring success, and the following year Guttman declared: 'Maybe one day there would be Olympics for the disabled.'

His dream took another step forward in 1952 when the gathering became an international event, as Dutch war veterans descended on Stoke Mandeville to compete alongside their British counterparts. The early competitions were also known as the Stoke Mandeville Games, but as participation increased it was at Rome 1960 where the inaugural Paralympic Games took place.

When they did, it was not only war veterans who were invited to compete, as the concept continued to evolve. It was a landmark moment for athletes with an impairment, and Guttman once again played an integral role, along with Antonia Maglio, the Director of the Spinal Centre in the Italian capital.

That first Paralympic Games was held from 18-25 September, six days after the curtain came down on the Olympic Games, with 400 athletes competing and 23 nations represented. Medals were up for grabs in 57 events, although at that stage it was only athletes in wheelchairs who took part.

Among the sports included on the competition programme in those early days were Snooker, Wheelchair Fencing (Foil or Sabre), Javelin and Precision Javelin, Shot Put, Indian Club Throwing, Basketball and Swimming (Freestyle, Breaststroke and Backstroke). Table Tennis (Singles and Doubles), Archery, Dartchery and Pentathlon (Archery, Swimming, Javelin, Shot

Sir Ludwig Guttman.

Put and Club Throwing) were also on show.

That inaugural gathering saw Rome host both the Olympic Games and Paralympic Games, and Tokyo followed suit four years later, with races for athletes using wheelchairs added, but it would be another 24 years before both Games were again held together in the same city.

In between, almost 1,000 athletes took part in the Paralympic Games in Heidelberg, West Germany, in 1972, with 43 countries represented and athletes with quadriplegic spinal injuries competing for the first time. Visually impaired athletes also staged demonstration events as the Paralympic Movement continued to develop. It was also in Heidelberg that the 100m Wheelchair event was first included in the Athletics competition programme.

Four years later, it was on to Toronto, and in Canada the Paralympic Games were opened up to more disability groups as participation reached a new high of over 1,600. There were 261 amputees and 187 visually impaired athletes competing for the first time – a significant landmark. As well as greater numbers, there were also more events added to the programme. Goalball, for example, was introduced as a demonstration

The early days of disability sport at Stoke Mandeville Hospital in Buckinghamshire.

event, while Rifle Shooting became a medal event. There were also new distances for the Athletics, with new events over 200 metres, 400m, 800m and 1500m added.

It was a sign of the increasing interest and popularity of the Paralympic Games that the Toronto showpiece was the first to be televised daily.

The Dutch city of Arnhem was selected to host the 1980 Games and a crowd of over 12,000 people attended the Opening Ceremony at the Papendal National Sports Centre. A total of 42 countries were represented as 1,973 athletes participated, including athletes using wheelchairs, amputees, visually impaired athletes and – making their debut – 125 athletes with cerebral palsy. Sitting Volleyball was also incorporated into the competition programme, with the host nation winning gold. Meanwhile, Goalball became a medal event for visually impaired athletes.

Uniquely, there were two hosts for for the 1984 Games, with athletes using wheelchairs competing at Stoke Mandeville in England, while visually impaired people and athletes with cerebral palsy competed at New York's Hofstra University.

At Seoul 1988, the profile of the Paralympic Games continued to grow, with several world records being broken – nine of which were achieved by American swimmer Trischa Zorn – as the world's best disabled athletes came together under the motto 'United for the Challenge'.

Increased television and media coverage helped to ensure that interest and awareness of the Paralympic Movement continued to grow rapidly, and the all-inclusive approach saw intellectually impaired athletes compete at Atlanta 1996, while in Sydney in 2000, Wheelchair Rugby was added to the programme as a full medal sport.

An amazing 1.2 million tickets were sold for the Sydney 2000 Games – the first in the Southern Hemisphere – with a record 123

countries competing. Athens 2004 and Beijing 2008 also saw a rise in the number of countries represented, and four years ago there were 472 medal events.

London 2012 promises to be even bigger and better, as more than 4,200 athletes prepare to compete in the country where Guttman first sowed the seeds for elite sport events for athletes with an impairment. More than 60 years on from his initial dream, the German doctor would be immensely proud of how far the Paralympic Games have come.

BELOW: The high-tech, modern approach in Beijing.

The London 2012 venues

Olympic Park venues

The Olympic Park forms the centrepiece of the Games. There are seven different venues in the Park, ranging from the state-of-the-art Olympic Stadium to the iconic Velodrome. Athletes will stay on-site in the Olympic and Paralympic Village.

Olympic Stadium

Sports and events: Athletics, Opening Ceremony, Closing Ceremony

The flagship venue for the London 2012 Games, the brand new Olympic Stadium will stage the Athletics events, as well as the Opening and Closing Ceremonies. With a stunning design that incorporates practicality with obvious aesthetic appeal, the stadium will be the focal point for this Games and one of London 2012's most visible legacies. Built with the environment in mind, the structure uses light steel and low-carbon concrete and is surrounded by water on three sides. Athletes will have an 80-metre warm-up track, top-of-the-range changing rooms and cutting-edge medical support facilities.

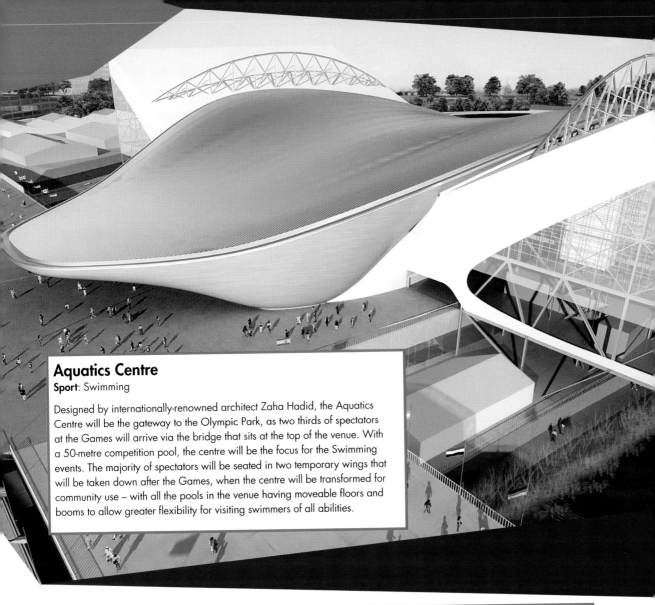

Aquatics Centre
Sport: Swimming

Designed by internationally-renowned architect Zaha Hadid, the Aquatics Centre will be the gateway to the Olympic Park, as two thirds of spectators at the Games will arrive via the bridge that sits at the top of the venue. With a 50-metre competition pool, the centre will be the focus for the Swimming events. The majority of spectators will be seated in two temporary wings that will be taken down after the Games, when the centre will be transformed for community use – with all the pools in the venue having moveable floors and booms to allow greater flexibility for visiting swimmers of all abilities.

Copper Box
Sport: Goalball

Located on the west side of the Olympic Park, the Copper Box will host the Goalball events. The facility, which features in excess of 3,000 square metres of external copper cladding, also has a distinctive multicoloured interior, while the concourse level is fully glazed to allow people in the Olympic Park to view the sport taking place inside. It will become a multi-use indoor arena for sport of all levels after the Games, with retractable seating.

Olympic Park continued overleaf

Basketball Arena

Sports: Wheelchair Basketball, Wheelchair Rugby

Located at the north end of the Olympic Park, the Basketball Arena will host Wheelchair Rugby and Wheelchair Basketball. The purpose-built arena is one of the largest temporary venues ever built for any Games and will be the fourth largest venue on the Olympic Park – occupying an area similar in size to two football pitches. Organisers will have just a couple of days to change over between the two sports the venue will host.

Velodrome

Sport: Cycling – Track

Designed with the help of four-time Olympic Games gold medallist Sir Chris Hoy, the Velodrome is intended to make optimum use of natural light and is the most sustainable venue in the Olympic Park. It is 100 per cent naturally ventilated to create the right track temperature and eliminate the need for air conditioning. The venue, which will form part of a new community-use VeloPark after the Games have finished, has a curved roof that perfectly compliments the shape of the track beneath it.

Riverbank Arena

Sports: Football (5-a-side, 7-a-side)

Once the Games are over, the Riverbank Arena will move further north to join with the Eton Manor facility. Once that change occurs, it will have 3,000 permanent seats, which could be increased by a further 12,000 for major events. For the first time in history, the Paralympic Games Football competitions will not be played on the traditional green coloured pitch, as the venue has been designed as a blue pitch with white lines.

Eton Manor

Sport: Wheelchair Tennis

The purpose-built arena at the north end of the Olympic Park is located on the site of the old Eton Manor Sports Club. Venue for the Wheelchair Tennis, there will be 13 courts in all – nine for competition and four for warm-up. Also part of the site are swimming pools which will be used by Aquatics competitors as a training facility. After the Games, the venue will be transformed into a facility for five-a-side football, hockey, tennis and wheelchair tennis.

Olympic and Paralympic Village

These apartments form part of the Olympic Park and have the capacity to house up to 17,000 athletes and officials. But despite the large numbers of guests, the Village still features large areas of open space throughout, with the courtyard areas in the middle of each residential block being the same size as four tennis courts. After the Games, the Village will be transformed into a new community in east London with 2,800 homes.

How to get there:
Tube – West Ham, Stratford;
Rail or Docklands Light Railway –
West Ham, Stratford,
Stratford International.

Other London venues

As well as the Olympic Park, the Games will be taking place at several other venues across London. Some are relatively new, such as the North Greenwich Arena, while some are centuries old, such as The Royal Artillery Barracks.

ExCeL

Sports: Boccia, Table Tennis, Judo, Powerlifting, Sitting Volleyball, Wheelchair Fencing

ExCeL will need no alterations to get it ready for London 2012, with the venue boasting top-class facilities that will see it able to host six sports.

How to get there: Docklands Light Railway – Custom House, West Silvertown Stations.

Greenwich Park

Sport: Equestrian

A temporary cross-country course has been designed in London's oldest Royal Park. On the banks of the River Thames, the park is a popular tourist hotspot, with The Royal Observatory nearby.

How to get there: Rail – Greenwich, Blackheath; Docklands Light Railway – Greenwich.

The Mall

Sport: Athletics – Marathon

A ceremonial route in the heart of London, access will be free for spectators, although some ticketing is available for certain popular areas.

How to get there: Tube – Victoria, St James' Park, Green Park; Rail – London Charing Cross, London Victoria, London Waterloo.

North Greenwich Arena

Sport: Wheelchair Basketball

Originally built in 1999 when it was known as the Millennium Dome, the North Greenwich Arena is a multi-purpose arena that will be one of the most iconic structures at London 2012.

How to get there: Tube – North Greenwich; Rail – Charlton Station.

The Royal Artillery Barracks

Sports: Archery, Shooting

In contrast to many of the newly-built Paralympic Games venues, The Royal Artillery Barracks in south-east London was opened in 1766.

How to get there: Docklands Light Railway or Rail – Woolwich Arsenal Station.

Venues outside London

London is the main focus of Paralympic action but it is not the only location involved in hosting the Games. Three major events will take place in world-class venues outside Greater London.

Brands Hatch, Kent

Sport: Cycling – Road

Famous as a motor racing circuit, Brands Hatch will be the focal point for the Road Race and Time Trial Cycling events and will form the base for half of the course – including the start and finish.

How to get there: Rail – Swanley Station.

Eton Dorney, Buckinghamshire

Sport: Rowing

To the west of London, near Windsor Castle, The 2,200-metre venue has an eight-lane rowing course and has already proved capable of hosting top-class events after staging the 2006 Rowing World Championships.

How to get there: Rail – Slough, Maidenhead, Windsor and Eton Riverside Stations.

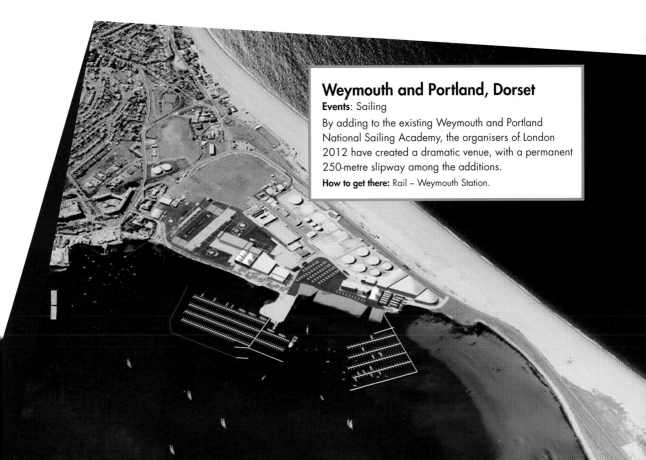

Weymouth and Portland, Dorset

Events: Sailing

By adding to the existing Weymouth and Portland National Sailing Academy, the organisers of London 2012 have created a dramatic venue, with a permanent 250-metre slipway among the additions.

How to get there: Rail – Weymouth Station.

Paralympic Games schedule

With 11 days of spectacular sport taking place, there is something for everyone at London 2012. This handy schedule shows you when and where to catch all the action, with each day broken down into individual sessions.

Sport	Venue
Opening Ceremony 29 August	Olympic Stadium, Olympic Park
Archery 30 August–5 September	The Royal Artillery Barracks, London
Athletics 31 August–8 September	Olympic Stadium, Olympic Park
Athletics – Marathon 9 September	The Mall, London
Boccia 2–8 September	ExCeL, London
Cycling – Road 5–8 September	Brands Hatch, Kent
Cycling – Track 30 August–2 September	Velodrome, Olympic Park
Equestrian 30 August–4 September	Greenwich Park, London
Football – 5-a-side 31 August–8 September	Riverbank Arena, Olympic Park
Football – 7-a-side 1–9 September	Riverbank Arena, Olympic Park
Goalball 30 August–7 September	Copper Box, Olympic Park
Judo 30 August–1 September	ExCeL, London
Powerlifting 30 August–5 September	ExCeL, London
Rowing 31 August–2 September	Eton Dorney, Buckinghamshire
Sailing 1–6 September	Weymouth and Portland, Dorset
Shooting 30 August–6 September	The Royal Artillery Barracks, London
Sitting Volleyball 30 August–8 September	ExCeL, London
Swimming 30 August–8 September	Aquatics Centre, Olympic Park
Table Tennis 30 August–8 September	ExCeL, London
Wheelchair Basketball 30 August–8 September	Basketball Arena, Olympic Park and North Greenwich Arena, London
Wheelchair Fencing 4–8 September	ExCeL, London
Wheelchair Rugby 5–9 September	Basketball Arena, Olympic Park
Wheelchair Tennis 1–8 September	Eton Manor, Olympic Park
Closing Ceremony 9 September	Olympic Stadium, Olympic Park

Session   Medal session

29 August	30 August	31 August	1 September	2 September	3 September	4 September	5 September	6 September	7 September	8 September	9 September
Wed	Thur	Fri	Sat	Sun	Mon	Tues	Wed	Thur	Fri	Sat	Sun

The events

When the first official Paralympic Games were held in Rome in 1960, just 400 athletes from 23 different countries competed in 57 medal events. Only athletes using wheelchairs were included at the landmark Games in the 'Eternal City', but 52 years on more than 4,000 athletes with a variety of impairments will descend on London. Across 11 days of competition there will be almost 300 sessions in 20 different sports, which range from the precision and skill of Paralympic Archery to the fast and frenetic action of Wheelchair Rugby. More than 2,100 medals will be presented during 503 Victory Ceremonies at 15 different competition venues.

High-speed action in the men's 200m – T54 semi-final at Beijing 2008.

Archery

There will be no shortage of drama and tension at The Royal Artillery Barracks in Woolwich as some of the most skilful individual competitors taking part in London 2012 go head-to-head for the Archery medals.

Archery has a rich history in the Paralympic Games. It was part of the Stoke Mandeville Games in 1948, the precursor to the modern Paralympic Movement, and featured in the first official event in Rome in 1960. It has formed an integral part of the programme ever since and came to worldwide attention when Paralympic archer Antonio Rebollo famously fired a flaming arrow to light the Olympic Cauldron and mark the start of the Barcelona 1992 showpiece.

Archery may be one of the most difficult sports to master but the objective is fairly straightforward, as competitors aim to fire their arrows as close as possible to the centre of a target that is 70 metres away from the shooting line.

The target is divided into 10 scoring circles, with the gold ring in the centre, which measures just 12.2 centimetres in diameter, being the hardest to hit and worth a maximum 10 points. Beyond that, the rings decrease in scoring value outwards towards the edge of the target.

Paralympic archers use two different types of bow to fire their arrows: recurve and compound. The main difference between the two is that the recurve bow has tips that curve away from the archer and are made with one string, while the compound bow has pulleys attached to the ends.

There will be three different types of competition on show at the 2012 Games – Individual Compound, Individual Recurve and a Team Recurve event. Archers in the individual competitions compete in a knockout format with matches played over five sets, each of which consists of three arrows per archer. The team competition is also a knockout event, but the matches take place between

Archers aim for a 12.2cm centre ring from a distance of 70m.

Key facts

Venue: The Royal Artillery Barracks, London

Dates: 30 August – 5 September

Current Paralympic champions:

Individual Compound – Open: John Stubbs (Great Britain, men's), Danielle Brown (Great Britain, women's)

Individual Compound – W1: David Drahonisky (Czech Republic)

Individual Recurve – Standing: Baatarjav Dambadondog (Mongolia, men's); Lee Hwa-Sook (South Korea, women's)

Individual Recurve – W1/W2: Cheng Changjie (China, men's); Gizem Girismen (Turkey, women's)

Team Recurve – Open: South Korea (men's), China (women's)

Star athlete: Danielle Brown

Born: 10/04/1988

Country: Great Britain

Event: Women's Individual Compound – Open

Classification: Standing

Paralympic Medals: Gold women's Individual Compound – Open (Beijing 2008)

Only five years after taking up the sport, Danielle Brown joined a select group of athletes to have won gold in their first Paralympic Games.

She had already triumphed in her first World Championships in 2007 before her Beijing success and followed that with gold in the World Championships again in 2009 and in 2011. She was also part of the England team that won the Team Compound event at the Commonwealth Games in Delhi.

having come second behind China four years ago.

The Chinese and South Koreans dominated the team events at Beijing 2008 and will doubtless be strong contenders for the medals once again this time around. In particular, look out for China's Fangxia Gao, who won silver in the women's Individual Recurve – Standing event four years ago and is the reigning world champion.

With 140 archers competing overall (88 men and 52 women) and nine gold medals at stake, there could be no grander setting for the Archery competition than The Royal Artillery Barracks in Woolwich. The construction on the current buildings began in 1776 and the venue has a rich heritage in the British military that will provide a fitting backdrop for the action.

teams of three archers facing off in a best-of-24 arrows format.

Archers are categorised into three classification groups depending on the extent of their physical impairment. Archers who compete in the Standing class have full use of their arms but their legs show some degree of loss of muscle strength, co-ordination and/or joint mobility. In this class, archers can either shoot from a standing position or sitting down on a stool.

Those in the W1 category use a wheelchair for mobility and also have an impairment that restricts the use of their arms and legs. Finally, archers in the W2 category have an impairment that affects their legs.

Archery requires equal amounts of skill, accuracy and strength, with matches often decided by only a few points. Concentration is key, as is a

steady nerve to continually hit the centre of the target. At the highest level, archers usually strike the centre ring, meaning that one stray arrow can often prove costly to medal hopes.

The most decorated archer at this level is Italy's Paola Fantato, who won an astonishing five gold, one silver and two bronze medals over the course of five Paralympic Games from Seoul 1988 to Athens 2004 and is widely recognised as one of the sport's finest athletes.

One woman who will certainly be looking to step into the limelight and follow in Fantato's footsteps this time around is Great Britain's Danielle Brown, who took gold in the women's Individual Compound – Open competition at the Beijing 2008 Games. Brown will head a Great Britain team that will be looking to top the medal table,

Classification categories

- **Standing** – Archers have full use of their arms and shoot from standing position or using a stool or chair
- **W1** – Archers have an impairment that affects their arms and legs
- **W2** – Archers have an impairment that affects their legs

Ones to watch

1. **John Stubbs** (men's Individual Compound – Open, Great Britain)
2. **Fangxia Gao** (women's Individual Recurve – Standing, China)
3. **Philippe Horner** (men's Individual Compound – Open, Switzerland)

Athletics
100m, 200m and 400m

The sprint events at the London 2012 Games are sure to be among the most popular, with big crowds expected to fill the Olympic Stadium to watch the fastest athletes in the world going for gold.

Athletics is steeped in history, dating back to ancient Greek times, and it will be the largest sport on the London 2012 programme. In the 100m, 200m and 400m alone there will be a total of 69 gold medal races as men and women compete separately in competitions for ambulent athletes and athletes using wheelchairs.

The 100m is an all-out sprint, with athletes looking to reach their top speed as quickly as possible. The 200m requires runners to hold their top pace for longer and also master the art of sprinting off a bend. Meanwhile, in the 400m an element of tactics is required in order to time the race perfectly and not burn out too early.

Due to the large number of events, Athletics also has the greatest number of classification categories. Every competitor is given a two-digit number, with the first indicating the nature of the athlete's impairment. The second number denotes the severity of their impairment – the lower the number the more severe the impairment.

Athletics was one of the earliest disability sports to be developed and it first appeared at the Stoke Mandeville 1952 Games. It was the first sprint to feature at a Paralympic Games at Tokyo 1964.

The sprint events for athletes using wheelchairs are often frenetic, with athletes reaching top speeds of around 30kph (19mph) or more. In addition,

Key facts

Venue: Olympic Stadium, London

Dates: 31 August – 8 September

Current Paralympic Champions:

100m Men: L.Prado (T11, Brazil), J.Jamison (T12, USA), J.Smyth (T13, Ireland), Y.Sen (T35, China), R.Pavlyk (T36, Ukraine), F.Van der Merwe (T37, South Africa), E.O'Hanlon (T38, Australia), E.Connor (T42, Canada), O.Pistorius (T44, South Africa), H.Francis (T46, Australia), D.Bergeron (T52, Canada), J.George (T53, USA), L.Tahti (T54, Finland)

100m Women: W.Chunmiao (T11, China), O.Boturchuk (T12, Ukraine), S.Benhama (T13, Morocco), W.Fang (T36, China), L.McIntosh (T37, USA), I.Dyachenko (T38, Ukraine), P.Bustamante (T42, Mexico), A.Holmes (T44, USA), Y.Castillo (T46, Cuba), M.Stilwell (T52, Canada), H.Lisha (T53, China), C.Petitclerc (T54, Canada)

200m Men: L.Prado (T11, Brazil), H.Langenhoven (T12, South Africa), J.Smyth (T13, Ireland), S.Wa Wai (T36, Hong Kong), F.Van der Merwe (T37, South Africa), E.O'Hanlon (T38, Australia), O.Pistorius (T44, South Africa), H.Francis (T46, Australia), D.Bergeron (T52, Canada), Y.Shiran (T53, China), Z.Lixin (T54, China)

200m Women: T.Guilhermina (T11, Brazil), A.El'Hannouni (T12, France), S.Benhama (T13, Morocco), W.Fang (T36, China), L.McIntosh (T37, USA), I.Dyachenko (T38, Ukraine), K.Green (T44, Germany), Y.Castillo (T46, Cuba), M.Stilwell (T52, Canada), C.Petitclerc (T54, Canada)

400m Men: L.Prado (T11, Brazil), L.Yansong (T12, China), L.Manuel Galano (T13, Cuba), R.Pavlyk (T36, Ukraine), F.Chida (T38, Tunisia), O.Pistorius (T44, South Africa), H.Francis (T46, Australia), T.Ito (T52, Japan), H.Suk-Man (T53, South Korea), Z.Lixin (T54, China)

400m Women: A.El'Hannouni (T12, France), S.Benhama (T13, Morocco), J.Galli (T53, USA), C.Petitclerc (T54, Canada)

Superstar Irish sprinter Jason Smyth.

Star athlete: Terezinha Guilhermina

Born: 03/10/1978

Country: Brazil

Events: Women's 100m and 200m – T11, women's 400m – T12

Classification: T11

Paralympic Medals: Bronze women's 400m – T12 (Athens 2004); Gold women's 200m – T11, Silver women's 100m – T11, Bronze women's 400m – T12 (Beijing 2008)

Terezinha Guilhermina (bottom) aims to defend her tag of 'The fastest female Paralympian in the world'.

Guilhermina, who runs with a guide runner, won her first Paralympic Games medal when she took bronze in the 400m – T12 event at Athens 2004. However, it was at Beijing 2008 where she came into her own, winning gold in the 200m and silver in the 100m – T11 events and also bronze in the 400m – T12. She went on to claim three golds at the 2011 IPC World Athletics Championships.

athletes who stray outside their designated lane are disqualified.

Rules vary in the races for athletes who do not require a wheelchair, depending on the class in which they compete. For example, in the sprint events for visually impaired athletes, blind competitors (T11) are aided by guide runners, while T12 athletes can have a guide run with them if they wish. The two are joined with a rope and two lanes are used by each pair.

Running with a guide is a skill in itself, with the duo required to run at exactly the same pace. This means that guide runners have to be as fit as the athletes they partner, and many are former sprinters themselves.

Irish runner Jason Smyth (see page 103) was the superstar of

the T13 sprint events at Beijing 2008, winning gold in the men's 100m and 200m and breaking the world record in both, making him the fastest Paralympian.

Smyth, who trains alongside American sprint star Tyson Gay, became the first disabled athlete to compete in the non-disabled European Championships in 2010 and also competed at the 2011 non-disabled World Championships.

As well as Smyth, there will be a major focus on the 100m, 200m and 400m – T44 events, where the most high-profile disabled athlete, Oscar Pistorius (see page 101), will be looking to defend his titles. Pistorius was born without fibulas in both of his legs and runs on carbon-fibre blades, which has earned

him the nickname of 'The Blade Runner'. The South African holds the world record in the 100m, 200m and 400m – T44 events and will be a strong favourite to achieve a hat-trick of gold medals in London. However, he will face strong opposition in the 100m in particular from Jerome Singleton of the United States, who pipped Pistorius to victory at the 2011 IPC World Athletics Championships in New Zealand.

The 100m – T44 for women was won by April Holmes at Beijing 2008 and the American world record holder will be a strong favourite again. Evan O'Hanlon of Australia is also a key contender in the T38 category. He broke the world record in both the 100m and 200m events at Beijing 2008 and also won a third gold in the T35-T38 4 x 100m Relay.

Classification categories

- **T11-T13** – Athletes with a visual impairment
- **T20** – Athletes with an intellectual impairment
- **T31-T38** – Athletes with co-ordination problems including cerebral palsy. Classes T31–T34 use a wheelchair to compete
- **T40-T46** – Athletes with a loss of limb or other limb impairment
- **T51-T54** – Wheelchair track athletes

Ones to watch

1. **Oscar Pistorius** (men's 100m, 200m and 400m – T44, South Africa)
2. **April Holmes** (women's 100m – T44, USA)
3. **Jason Smyth** (men's 100m – T13 and 200m – T13, Ireland)

Kurt Fearnley races to his second gold medal
The men's Marathon (T54 Wheelchair category) speeds
along the streets of Beijing during the 2008 Paralympic
Games. With the athletes slipstreaming each other, the
Australian Kurt Fearnley (second right) stays out of trouble at the
front of the pack before going on to win his second consecutive
Marathon gold in the T54 category. His winning time was
1:22:17, more than 44 minutes quicker than the non-disabled
men's Marathon winning time.

Full of high drama and plenty of excitement, the relay races are some of the highlights of the Athletics programme and the finals are sure to be among the most popular with spectators at the Olympic Stadium.

Each team is made up of four athletes, who all run a leg of the race before passing a baton over to the next team-mate. The final athlete carries the baton to the finish line.

The relay races will provide some of the most intense competition at the Games, and they have featured on the programme since Athletics track events were first introduced at Tokyo 1964. Back then, two races were competed for by male athletes in wheelchairs. At the Tel Aviv 1968 Games, a single 4 x 40m wheelchair race was held for men and women.

The first men's 4 x 100m Relays featured at Toronto 1976, with races over 400m for male athletes being added at Arnhem 1980. It was not until the Games four years later, held in New York and Stoke Mandeville, that the ambulent events for women were included, and at London 2012 there will be a total of four

relay races – two 4 x 100m and one 4 x 400m event for men and a single 4 x 100m race for women – all of which are sure to capture the imagination of the crowd.

Much like the individual 100m events, the 4 x 100m is all about speed but, crucially, a clean changeover of the baton is arguably the most important key to success. With athletes travelling at full speed,

Sprint superstar Oscar Pistorius.

passing the baton cleanly is a tough task, especially as the changeover must be completed within a clearly-marked zone. If the baton is not passed on inside the takeover box then the whole team is disqualified. For that reason, teams train just as hard on perfecting smooth changeovers as they do on honing their raw speed. Athletes are not disqualified if they drop the baton, providing they do not impede another runner when retrieving it.

Given the wide range of athletes competing, each event has specific rules depending on its classification, which are set out by the International Paralympic Committee (IPC). For example, the 4 x 100m Relay – T11-T13 is contested by athletes with visual impairments. The T11 athletes are the most affected by their visual impairments and run with a guide runner, while T12 athletes can use a guide if they wish and T13 athletes run unaided.

The rules for this event require that each team must consist of at least one T11 and T12 athlete and no more than one T13 runner. The baton can be carried and passed over by either the athlete or the guide, but it must be done so within the permitted zone and the athlete and guide must be within 0.5 metres of each other.

Key facts

Venue: Olympic Stadium, London

Dates: 4-8 September

Current Paralympic champions:
4 x 100m Relay – T11-T13: China
4 x 100m Relay – T35-T38: N/A
4 x 100m Relay – T42-T46: USA
4 x 400m Relay – T53/T54: China

Event: 4 x 100m Relay – T42-T46

Paralympic Medals: Bronze 4 x 100m Relay – T42-T46 (Atlanta 1996), Gold 4 x 100m Relay – T42-T46 (Athens 2004), Gold 4 x 100m Relay – T42-T46 (Beijing 2008)

The United States will undoubtedly be strong challengers for another gold medal in the 4 x 100m Relay – T42-T46 at London 2012. They could only take bronze on home soil at the Atlanta 1996 Games but have dominated the event in recent years, winning gold at Athens 2004 and again in Beijing four years ago, when they broke the world record with a time of 42.75.

London 2012 is likely to throw up another showdown between USA's Jerome Singleton and Oscar Pistorius, who was beaten in the individual 100m for the first time in seven years by the American in 2011.

Spain have traditionally performed well in the 4 x 100m Relays for visually impaired athletes, winning gold at Barcelona 1992, Atlanta 1996 and bronze at Sydney 2000. However, China have emerged more recently as a dominant nation and won gold at the Athens 2004 Games, before defending their title four years ago at Beijing 2008.

Athletes with a loss of limb or other limb impairment will compete in the 4 x 100m Relay – T42-T46. In this event, each team is allowed no more than two T46 runners, who have single arm above or below elbow amputations. The changeover is completed by just touching their team-mate.

The United States won gold at Athens 2004 and retained their title at the Beijing 2008 Games,

while Brazil are also a strong team. With the inspirational Oscar Pistorius in their line-up, South Africa edged out the USA to win gold at the 2011 IPC World Athletics Championships in New Zealand and will once again expect to be in contention for the medals.

London 2012 will be the first time that the 4 x 100m Relay – T35-T38 women's race has been contested at a Paralympic Games. Ukraine will be one of the favourites.

The solitary 4 x 400m Relay race will be for T53/T54 athletes and the changeover is completed via a touch on the outgoing athlete, while each team must include at least one T53 competitor in their line-up. China won the event at Beijing 2008 and then took gold at the 2011 World Championships.

Athletics
800m and 1500m

While the sprint events are all about raw speed and power, in the middle-distance races athletes must combine that pace with endurance and stamina, while tactics also play an important role.

Races over 800m cover two laps of the track and the 1500m is over three-and-three-quarter laps, with both events placing unique demands on competitors. Unlike the sprint events, athletes do not stay in lane for the entire race and instead come together to form a pack. For that reason, tactics are extremely important in middle-distance racing and often mean the difference between going home with a medal or not.

Athletes will be looking to pace their race and time their final burst for the line perfectly in order to avoid using up their energy too soon.

Athletics has a prestigious history but it was not until Toronto 1976 that the 800m and 1500m events first appeared on the competition programme at the Paralympic Games. As the classification system has been broken down over the years, more events have been added, and at London 2012 there will be a total of 10 categories at 800m and nine 1500m gold medals up for grabs.

Over the course of Paralympic Games history some of the greatest 800m and 1500m athletes have come from the T51-T54 class. Canada's Chantal Petitclerc won an astonishing 14 gold, five silver and two bronze medals during her illustrious career to become the most successful female in the history of Athletics at the Paralympic Games. Three of those gold medals came in the 800m – T54 and two in the 1500m – T54 event, and she was the champion at both distances at Beijing 2008.

However, those Games in China were Petitclerc's last major international event before she retired and the likes of fellow Canadian Diane Roy and American Tatyana McFadden will be looking to take her crown this time around. McFadden in particular is being tipped to be one of the stars of London 2012 having emerged as a dominant force in Athletics in the run up to the Games.

In the men's 800m – T54 and 1500m – T54 events, Great Britain's David Weir is one of the outstanding performers, and he will be looking to retain the gold medals he won four years ago, although he will face strong competition from Switzerland's Marcel Hug – who has broken the world record over both these distances.

In the 1500m – T11 event, visually impaired athletes will run with a guide runner to help them around the track. The guide runner must match the

Key facts

Venue: Olympic Stadium, London

Dates: 31 August – 8 September

Current Paralympic champions:

Men's 800m: Abderrahim Zhiou (T12, Tunisia), Abdelilah Marne (T13, Morocco), Artem Arefyev (T36, Russia), Michael McKillop (T37, Ireland), Marcin Awizen (T46, Poland), Tomoya Ito (T52, Japan), Li Huzhao (T53, China), Zhou Hongzhuan (T53, China), David Weir (T54, Great Britain)

Women's 800m: Chantal Petitclerc (T54, Canada)

Men's 1500m: Zhang Zhen (T11, China), Henry Kirwa (T13, Kenya), Abraham Cheruiyot Tarbei (T46, Kenya), David Weir (T54, Great Britain)

Women's 1500m: Chantal Petitclerc (T54, Canada)

Double gold medallist David Weir.

Star athlete:
Tatyana McFadden

Born: 21/04/1989

Country: USA

Events: Women's 800m – T54 and 1500m – T54

Classification: T54

Paralympic Medals: Silver Women's 100m – T54, Bronze women's 200m – T54 (Athens 2004); Silver women's 200m – T54, 400m – T54 and 800m – T54 (Beijing 2008)

Tatyana McFadden looks set to cement her reputation as one of the top athletes at London 2012. She won silver in the 100m and bronze in the 200m on her debut in 2004, behind Chantal Petitclerc.

The American had to settle for silver in the 200m, 400m and 800m again at Beijing 2008 but with her rival now retired, McFadden is ready to take on Petitclerc's crown.

athlete's stamina and the pair need a good understanding in order to run at the same pace. Athletes must also cross the finish line before their guide runner, otherwise they will be disqualified.

Brazil's Odair Santos broke the world record to win 1500m gold in the T11 class at the 2011 IPC World Athletics Championships in New Zealand, and he will be among the favourites for the gold medal again.

Meanwhile, the T37 events, for athletes with cerebral palsy, are also likely to be fiercely contested. Irishman Michael McKillop looks to be the man to beat in that class after following up his gold medal in the 800m at the Beijing 2008 Games by breaking his own world record to retain his title at the World Championships last year.

The 1500m – T37 was not on the competition programme in Beijing 2008, but it is back for London 2012 and McKillop is also expected to feature prominently in that.

The London 2012 Games will mark the return of events for intellectually impaired athletes after a 12-year absence.

They first competed at Seoul 1988 but have not featured since Sydney 2000 due to difficulties in determining the eligibility of competitors. However, in 2009 the International Paralympic Committee (IPC) voted to re-admit them and there will be a 1500m event for both men and women at London 2012.

Peyman Nasiri of Iran won the men's title and Poland's Arleta Meloch was crowned women's 1500m – T20 champion at the World Athletics Championships and both will be looking to make their mark on an even bigger stage here.

Classification categories

- **T11-T13** – Athletes with a visual impairment
- **T20** – Athletes with an intellectual impairment
- **T31-T38** – Athletes with co-ordination problems including cerebral palsy. Classes T31-T34 use a wheelchair to compete
- **T40-T46** – Athletes with a loss of limb or other limb impairment
- **T51-T54** – Wheelchair track athletes

Ones to watch

1. **Michael McKillop** (800m – T37 and 1500m – T37, Ireland)
2. **David Weir** (men's 800m – T54 and 1500m – T54, Great Britain)
3. **Odair Santos** (men's 1500m – T11, Brazil)

Athletics
5000m

The 5000m is the longest track event that will be contested at the London 2012 Games and is sure to test the athletes' stamina and strength to the full over a gruelling 12-and-a-half-lap race.

Star athlete: Odair Santos

Born: 17/05/1981

Country: Brazil

Event: Men's 5000m – T11

Classification Category: T11

Paralympic Medals: Silver men's 1500m – T12 and men's 5000m – T12, Bronze men's 800m – T12 (Athens 2004); Bronze men's 800m – T12, men's 5000m – T13 and men's 10,000m – T12 (Beijing 2008)

Santos (in green, above) has won two silvers and four bronzes from the last two Games but is likely to arrive with high hopes of gold this time after winning the 1500m – T11, 5000m – T11 and 10,000m – T11 titles at the IPC World Athletics Championships last year.

The event was not included in the Paralympic Games until Arnhem 1980, where it appeared in the form of two walk competitions for male athletes only. However, the 5000m played a more prominent part four years later at the Stoke Mandeville and New York 1984 Games, where there were medals contested in nine events for male athletes and four for women.

The number of classification categories has since been reduced, and at London 2012 there will be two races for visually impaired male athletes, in the T11 and T12 classes, and a separate race for both men and women in the T54 class for athletes using wheelchairs.

China's Zhen Zhang won gold in the 5000m – T11 at Beijing 2008, but Brazil's Odair Santos looks to be the man to beat this time after he won the title at the 2011 IPC Athletics World Championships. Meanwhile, the 5000m – T12 event is back again this year after being omitted from the competition programme in Beijing.

Athletes in the T54 events will have to call on all of their skill in order to avoid the crashes that have sometimes resulted in the past in races using wheelchairs, with athletes hitting top speeds of around 30kph (19mph). In fact, the women's 5000m – T54

race at Beijing 2008 had to be re-started after a crash on the penultimate lap. Amanda McGrory of the USA went on to take gold. Switzerland's Marcel Hug holds the world record in the men's 5000m – T54 event.

Key facts

Venue: Olympic Stadium, London

Dates: 31 August – 7 September

Current Paralympic champions:
Men: Zhen Zhang (T11, China), Prawat Wahoram (T54, Malaysia)
Women: Amanda McGrory (T54, USA)

Classification categories

- **T11-T13** – Athletes with a visual impairment
- **T40-T46** – Athletes with a loss of limb or other limb impairment
- **T51-T54** – Wheelchair track athletes

Ones to watch

1. **Marcel Hug** (men's 5000m – T54, Switzerland)
2. **Shelly Woods** (women's 5000m – T54, Great Britain)
3. **Henry Kirwa** (men's 5000m – T12, Kenya)

Athletics
Marathon

The streets of London will provide a scenic backdrop as the elite athletes battle it out in what is widely considered to be the most demanding test of endurance at the Paralympic Games – the Marathon.

Star athlete: Kurt Fearnley

Born: 23/03/1981

Country: Australia

Event: Men's Marathon – T54

Classification: T54

Paralympic Medals: Silver men's 800m – T54 and men's 4 x 100m Relay – T53-T54 (Sydney 2000); Gold men's 5000m – T54 and men's Marathon – T54, Silver men's 4 x 100m Relay – T53-T54 (Athens 2004); Gold men's Marathon – T54, Silver men's 5000m – T54 and men's 800m – T54 Bronze men's 1500m – T54 (Beijing 2008)

Kurt Fearnley is a Marathon great. After making his Games debut at 19 at Sydney 2000, his domination began with gold at Athens 2004, a title he retained at Beijing 2008.

He has also won in New York, London, Chicago, Los Angeles, Seoul, Rome, Paris and Sydney.

Traditionally, the Marathon has finished inside the main stadium, but the route at London 2012 will see competitors start and finish in The Mall.

Athletes will race around a loop circuit past sights such as Buckingham Palace, Admiralty Arch, Birdcage Walk, St Paul's Cathedral, Tower Hill and the Houses of Parliament before entering the finishing straight.

There will be four gold medals up for grabs, with separate events for men and women in the T54 wheelchair class, while there are also events for men in the T12 (visually impaired) and T46 (athletes with a loss of limb or other limb impairment) classes.

Marathon events were first introduced for athletes using wheelchairs at Stoke Mandeville and New York 1984.

The men's Marathon – T54 race is sure to be a compelling one. Australia's Kurt Fearnley is the defending champion after claiming victory at Beijing 2008 and he will be confident of more success. Fearnley also won gold at the Athens 2004 Games, while the biggest challenge to his hat-trick is likely to come from Great Britain's David Weir and Switzerland's Marcel Hug. Weir won his fifth London Marathon in 2011, while Hug has broken the world record for all races from 800m to 10,000m. The Marathon – T46 event should see a return for Mario Santillan, who broke the world record at Beijing 2008, while in the T12 event China's Shun Qi also broke the world record four years ago before Alberto Suarez Laso later bettered his time.

Key facts

Venue: The Mall, London

Date: 9 September

Current Paralympic champions:
Men: Shun Qi (T12, China), Mario Santillan (T46, Mexico), Kurt Fearnley (T54, Australia)
Women: Edith Hunkeler (T54, Switzerland)

Classification categories

- T11-T13 – Athletes with a visual impairment
- T40-T46 – Athletes with a loss of limb or other limb impairment
- T51-T54 – Athletes who compete in a wheelchair

Ones to watch

1. **Mario Santillan** (Marathon – T46, Mexico)
2. **Alberto Suarez Laso** (Marathon – T12, Spain)
3. **David Weir** (men's Marathon – T54, Great Britain)

Throwing events were the basis in Athletics of the first-ever Paralympic Games in Rome in 1960 and there will be medals up for grabs in four throwing disciplines – Club, Discus, Javelin and Shot Put – this time around.

In total, there will be 52 gold medals to compete for across the programme, with the combination of strength and skill on show set to delight spectators.

Of the 25 events that made up the competition programme at Rome 1960, all but one were throwing competitions, as male and female athletes battled it out in the Shot Put, Club Throw and Javelin Throw, while there was also a Precision Javelin event. Early success belonged to Great Britain's Dick Thompson, who took four gold medals. Italy's Maria Scutti dominated the women's events and produced a remarkable performance to take nine of the 12 gold medals on offer in those four field events.

This year's winners are likely to be far more varied and, depending on their impairment, athletes will compete either standing up or sitting down. Seated athletes compete in specially-adapted throwing frames or chairs, which give them extra support.

The throwing disciplines have both single-classification events and combined events for athletes with differing levels of impairment. In the single-classification events, the athlete who throws the furthest is the winner. However, in mixed-classification events the Raza System is used to determine an overall point score.

The Raza System was developed in 2010 and uses statistical analysis to give a comparison of athletes' performances, independent of their classification or other event-specific criteria. Under the system, the athlete with the most points at the end of the competition when all the factors are taken into account wins, meaning that it is not always the athlete who throws the furthest that takes gold.

In simple terms, however, the throwing events remain straightforward – with the aim

Key facts

Venue: Olympic Stadium, London

Dates: 31 August – 8 September

Current Paralympic champions:

Men's Discus Throw: Wei Guo (F35/F36, China), Javad Hardani (F37/F38, Iran), Fanie Lombard (F42, South Africa), Jeremy Campbell (F44, USA), Alexey Ashapatov (F57/F58, Russia)

Women's Discus Throw: Qing Wu (F35/F36, China), Jimisu Menggen (F40, China), Eucharia Njideka Iyaizi (F57/F58, Nigeria)

Men's Javelin Throw: Mohammad Reza Mirzaei Jaberi (F57/F58, Iran)

Women's Javelin Throw: Antonia Balek (F33/F34/F52/F53, Croatia), Martina Monika Willing (F54/F55/F56, Germany), Supin Qing (F57/F58, China)

Men's Shot Put: David Casinos (F11/F12, Spain), Dong Xia (F37/F38, China), Paschalis Stathelakos (F40, Greece), Alexey Ashapatov (F57/F58, Russia)

Women's Shot Put: Alla Malchyk (F35/F36, Ukraine), Raoua Tlili (F40, Tunisia), Eva Kacanu (F54/F55/F56, Czech Republic), Eucharia Njideka Iyaizi (F57/F58, Nigeria)

Men's Club Throw F31/F32/F51: N/A

Women's Club Throw F31/F32/F51: N/A

Tunisia's Shot Put champion Raoua Tlili.

Star athlete: Daniel Greaves

Born: 04/10/1982

Country: Great Britain

Event: Discus Throw – F44

Classification: F44

Paralympic Medals: Silver Discus Throw – F44/F46 (Sydney 2000), Gold Discus Throw – F44/F46 (Athens 2004), Bronze Discus Throw – F44 (Beijing 2008)

Daniel Greaves goes into the London 2012 Games looking to prove a point in front of a passionate home crowd. Greaves was just 17 when he won a silver medal at Sydney 2000 and four years later he broke the world record in Athens. Much was expected of him at Beijing 2008, but he had to settle for a bronze medal.

Fuelled by that disappointment, Greaves has bounced back and produced consistent performances.

He broke the world record when he won gold in the Discus Throw – F44 at the 2011 World Championships and beat that mark again a few months later at the BT Paralympic World Cup.

being to launch the chosen object as far as possible.

In the Javelin Throw, male athletes use a spear of between 2.6-2.7 metres in length, while for women the spear is 2.2-2.3m. Upper-body strength is essential for any javelin thrower, with standing athletes launching the spear from the end of a runway and using a run-up to build-up speed, while sitting athletes launch the javelin into the air from a seated position.

Iran's Mohammad Reza Mirzaei Jaberi has won three out of the last four gold medals in the Javelin Throw, culminating with victory in the F57/F58 category at Beijing 2008, while Brazilian Shirlene Coelho will be looking to follow

up her World Championships success in the F37/F38 class.

The Discus Throw is steeped in history and was one of the sports in the ancient Pentathlon, which can be dated back to 708 BC. It did not feature at the first Paralympic Games but was introduced in Tokyo in 1964.

In this event, athletes throw a disc using a spinning motion. The technique varies for seated competition, but the aim is still to release the disc at the optimum moment to allow it to travel as far as possible. All Discus competitions take place inside a throwing cage for safety while visually impaired athletes in the F11 and F12 classes are permitted to bring one person

onto the field with them to act as a caller or guide.

In the Shot Put, athletes release a heavy metal ball, propelling it forward with as much power as possible from the base of the neck. Tunisia's Raoua Tlili has dominated the Shot Put – F40 competition for women over recent years, breaking the world record to win gold at Beijing 2008 before claiming another success at the 2011 World Championships, and she is once again expected to be in the hunt for medals.

Athletes competing in the Club Throw launch a club that weighs a minimum of 397 grams. London 2012 will see two new Club Throw champions crowned, with a combined F31/F32/F51 competition for men and a separate event for women appearing for the first time at these Games.

Classification categories

- **F11-F13** – Athletes with a visual impairment
- **F20** – Athletes with an intellectual impairment
- **F31-F38** – Athletes with co-ordination problems including cerebral palsy. Classes 31–34 use a wheelchair to compete
- **F40-F46** – Athletes with a loss of limb or other limb impairment
- **F51-F58** – Athletes who throw from a seated position

Ones to watch

1. **Shirlene Coelho** (Javelin Throw – F37/F38, Brazil)
2. **Nathan Stephens** (men's Javelin Throw – F57/F58, Great Britain)
3. **Raoua Tlili** (women's Shot Put – F40, Tunisia)

Athletics
Jumps

The jumping competitions will test athletes' speed and agility, with large crowds expected to flock to the Olympic Stadium to watch the action unfold across three different types of event – the Long Jump, High Jump and Triple Jump.

Each competition is held over a series of jumps and the gradual build-up to what is often a dramatic climax keeps the crowd on the edge of their seats.

Athletics has been part of every Paralympic Games but it was not until Toronto 1976 that the jump competitions were introduced, with seven High Jump events for men and two for women starting the trend.

In the High Jump, athletes run towards a raised bar and attempt to clear it without knocking it off. Before the competition, a Chief Judge decides a series of heights that the athletes can try to clear and they have three attempts to do so. A competitor is permitted to skip to one of the more challenging heights, however they cannot move forward again until they have cleared the bar at that height.

There will be two High Jump competitions for men at London 2012, in the F42 and F46 categories. F42 athletes have a single above or through knee amputation or an equivalent impairment. Athletes in the F46 class have a single above or below elbow amputation.

The only High Jump event at the Beijing 2008 Games was a combined men's F44/F46 competition, so two new champions will be crowned at London 2012. In the F42 class, China's Weizhong Guo will

be among the favourites after winning gold at the 2011 IPC World Athletics Championships in Christchurch, New Zealand. Meanwhile, Jeff Skiba of the USA won gold in the F44/F46 four years ago and also took world silver. Skiba will face strong competition from Poland's Maciej Lepiato, who pipped him to gold in New Zealand.

Building up speed is vital in the Long Jump, as athletes sprint down a runway before reaching a take-off board, which they use to try to propel themselves as far as possible down the landing area. Like the High Jump, the Long Jump was first introduced at Toronto 1976 and it has remained a fixture in the

Key facts

Venue: Olympic Stadium, London

Dates: 31 August – 8 September

Current Paralympic champions:
Men's High Jump F44/F46: Jeff Skiba (USA)
Men's Long Jump: Li Duan (F11, China), Farhat Chida (F37/F38, Tunisia), Wojtek Czyz (F42/F44, Poland), Arnaud Assoumani (F46, France)
Women's Long Jump: Ilse Hayes (F13, South Africa)
Men's Triple Jump: Li Duan (F11, China), Osamah Alshanqiti (F12, Saudi Arabia)

American Jeff Skiba on his way to a gold medal in the High Jump at Beijing 2008.

Athletics programme at every Games since. Athletes with the most severe visual impairment in the F11 class are permitted to be accompanied by two people to assist them with their positioning on the runway and act as callers to help guide them during the approach run.

In Long Jump events, if more than eight athletes are competing there is a preliminary round consisting of three attempts. The eight athletes who jump furthest progress to a final, in which they have six attempts. For single-class events, the athlete with the furthest jump in the final wins. In combined-class events, such as the F37/F38 class, the medals are decided using the Raza System – a statistical analysis method employed by the International Paralympic Committee (IPC) that compares athletes' performances independent of their classification and awards points based on the outcome.

Classification categories

- **F11-F13** – Athletes with a visual impairment
- **F20** – Athletes with an intellectual impairment
- **F31-F38** – Athletes with co-ordination problems including cerebral palsy
- **F40-F46** – Athletes with a loss of limb or other limb impairment

Ones to watch

1. **Arnaud Assoumani** (men's Long Jump – F46, France)
2. **Kelly Cartwright** (women's Long Jump – F24/F44, Australia)
3. **Weizhong Guo** (High Jump – F42, China)

Star athlete: Li Duan

Born: 04/05/1978

Country: China

Events: Long Jump – F11, Triple Jump – F11

Classification: F11

Paralympic Medals: Silver Triple Jump – F11, Bronze Long Jump – F11 (Sydney 2000); Gold Triple Jump – F11 and Long Jump – F11 (Athens 2004); Gold Triple Jump – F11 and Long Jump – F11 (Beijing 2008)

China's Li Duan has emerged as the king of the jump competitions for male F11 athletes. Duan made his Paralympic Games debut at Sydney 2000 and showed a glimpse of what was to come with a silver medal in the Triple Jump and bronze in the Long Jump.

At Athens 2004, he made the breakthrough as the top F11 jumper in the world with gold in both competitions, setting a Paralympic Games record in the Triple Jump in the process.

Much was expected of Duan in front of his home crowd at Beijing 2008 and he did not disappoint, breaking the world record on the way to retaining his Triple Jump title and winning another gold medal in the Long Jump.

The athlete with the most points is the winner.

Great Britain's Stefanie Reid broke the Long Jump – F44 world record in August 2010 and will carry home hopes in the women's F42/F44 competition. However, she is likely to face stiff competition from Australian Kelly Cartwright, who is the current world champion.

The Triple Jump, meanwhile, is the most technical of the jump competitions, with athletes required to perform a hop, skip and then a jump from the take-off board into the landing area. It was the last of the jump competitions to be introduced at the Paralympic Games and did not appear until Arnhem 1980, where there were two events for men. There has never been a Triple Jump competition held for female athletes.

Three gold medals will be up for grabs in the Triple Jump competition at London 2012, in the F11, F12 and F46 classes, with athletes having six attempts in the final and the furthest jump winning the gold medal.

Li Duan launches himself to glory in Beijing

The Beijing 2008 Paralympic Games cemented Li Duan's position as the best jumper in the world in the F11 category. Double gold at Athens 2004 in the Long Jump and Triple Jump (including a Paralympic Games record leap in the Triple Jump) was matched by two more golds in the same events four years later on home soil in China, where he went one better in the Triple Jump by setting a world record of 13.71 metres. If he stays fit, not many would bet against him for London 2012.

Boccia

A true test of an athlete's technique, nerve and their ability to concentrate under pressure, Boccia will be making an appearance as part of the Paralympic Games competition programme for the eighth time at London 2012.

The sport has been contested ever since the Stoke Mandeville and New York 1984 Games, where there were five medal events held in total – two for men, two for women and one mixed event, where men and women competed together. Since then, all Boccia events at the Paralympic Games have been mixed.

Played either individually, in pairs or in teams, the sport involves competitors taking turns to propel a ball down a rectangular court which measures 12.5 x 6 metres so that it lands as close as possible to a smaller white target ball, known as the 'jack'. Each player or team gets six balls to throw, with points scored for each one

that is closer to the jack than an opponent's at the culmination of each set of throws, known as an 'end'.

Individual and pairs matches consist of four ends in total, while team events are played out over six, with the most points scored ultimately winning.

Boccia is played by athletes with cerebral palsy using wheelchairs who are required to be in a seated position within a throwing box at one end of the court when they take their turn.

One of the key elements of success in this most skilled of sports is a combination of accuracy and tactical awareness, with players required to perform under pressure and show shrewd

tactical judgment to get the better of their opponents.

Games are often won by just a few points after the culmination of all the ends, so Boccia is as much a test of nerve as it is a judge of technique, particularly as the tension rises in the critical closing stages of a match.

When playing Boccia at national or international level, athletes compete in events with different classifications, based on their specific level of physical impairment. The BC1 category, made up of athletes with cerebral palsy whose impairment restricts their movement, use their hands and feet to propel the ball into play, and may be assisted by an aide. Those in the BC2 class may not be an

Key facts

Venues: ExCeL, London

Dates: 2–8 September

Current Paralympic champions:

Individual – BC1: Joao Paulo Fernandes (Portugal)

Individual – BC2: Hoi Ying Karen Kwok (South Korea)

Individual – BC3: Keon Woo-Park (South Korea)

Individual – BC4: Dirceu Pinto (Brazil)

Pairs – BC3: South Korea

Pairs – BC4: Brazil

Team – BC1/BC2: Great Britain

South Korea's Jeong Ho-won in action in the Beijing 2008 Boccia competition.

Star athlete: Nigel Murray

Born: 22/05/1964

Country: Great Britain

Events: Individual – BC2, Team – BC1/BC2

Classification: BC2

Paralympic Medals: Gold Individual – BC2 (Sydney 2000); Gold Team – BC1/BC2, Silver Individual – BC2 (Beijing 2008)

Nigel Murray became Great Britain's first Boccia gold medallist at Sydney 2000 – only 18 months after taking up the sport.

That success in the Individual – BC2 was followed by an individual silver at Beijing 2008, where he also captained the Great Britain team that won gold in the Team – BC1/BC2.

Murray has had a lengthy spell as world number one in the BC2 class, but will face tough competition from South Korea's Hoi Ying Karen Kwok, who beat him to the gold medal at Beijing 2008.

are expected to once again challenge four years on. Home hopes are also likely to be high, with Great Britain among the leading nations to compete in the sport, particularly when it comes to the high-profile team event. Led by world number one Nigel Murray, the British team claimed the gold medal in the Team – BC1/BC2 class at Beijing 2008 and will be strong challengers to defend their title this time around.

Look out also for the Brazilians, who have one of the sport's leading stars in the shape of Dirceu Pinto, the current Individual – BC4 World Champion, who claimed gold at Beijing 2008.

Classification categories

- **BC1** – Athletes with cerebral palsy who can either kick or throw the ball but their impairment has a significant impact on their ability to do so
- **BC2** – Athletes with cerebral palsy who find it easier to throw than BC1, but their impairment impacts on their ability to do so
- **BC3** – Athletes with any physical impairment who cannot independently kick or throw the ball three metres, and who therefore use a ramp
- **BC4** – Athletes with an impairment other than cerebral palsy who have difficulty throwing

assisted by an aide. Athletes with either cerebral palsy or any impairment preventing them kicking or throwing the ball are classified in the BC3 category and use a ramp to propel the ball into play, assisted by an aide. The final, BC4, category classifies those athletes who do not have cerebral palsy but have some other impairment and use their hands to propel the ball into play, without the support of an aide. In total, there will be seven Boccia gold medals up for grabs at London 2012, with the four individual events being prominent on the competition programme along with the pairs events and team competitions.

Each National Paralympic Committee (NPC) can have up to nine competing athletes in the

team and pairs events – made up of one team of four, one pair of three and another pair of two – and 12 competing athletes in the individual events, with qualification for a place at the Games determined by a competitor's placing in the Individual World Ranking List.

With the sport played in more than 50 countries worldwide and believed to have its origins dating all the way back to ancient Greece, competition for gold at London 2012 is sure to be intense, with Portugal likely to be among the favourites to claim medal honours. They topped the table for the total number of Boccia medals at the Beijing 2008 Games after completing a haul of one gold, three silver and one bronze and

Ones to watch

1. **Joao Paulo Fernandes** (Individual – BC1, Portugal)
2. **Hoi Ying Karen Kwok** (Individual – BC2, South Korea)
3. **Dirceu Pinto** (Individual – BC4, Brazil)

Cycling
Track

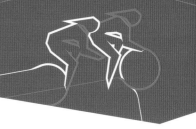

London 2012 will see host nation Great Britain aim to continue its recent domination of the Track Cycling events and claim more medals in front of an expectant home crowd at the impressive new Velodrome.

Great Britain won 12 of the 21 gold medals on offer across both the men's and women's competitions in Beijing four years ago, with Darren Kenny leading the way by claiming a trio of Paralympic Games titles in the Individual Pursuit, 1km Time Trial and Team Sprint events.

The next most successful nation, Australia, managed just four golds, and the majority of the sell-out crowds that are expected to witness the action this year will have high hopes that Team GB can continue their winning run four years on.

Track Cycling was included as part of the Paralympic Games competition programme for the first time in Atlanta in 1996. Seven different nations won at least one of the 11 gold medals on offer that year, before in Sydney four years later the hosts, Australia, led the way with a total haul of five golds.

In those early days, all events consisted entirely of tandem races – in which a blind or visually impaired athlete would take their place at the back and was joined by a non-disabled team-mate, who sat at the front and piloted the bike.

However, following Sydney 2000 the sport developed its technologies sufficiently to open itself up to a wider range of athletes, meaning that the Track Cycling programme was significantly increased in time for Athens 2004.

The London 2012 Track Cycling competition programme will consist of 18 events in total, with athletes split into categories according to their level of impairment. The two primary classification categories used in the Paralympic Track Cycling events are B for the blind or visually impaired and C for athletes with cerebral palsy, limb impairments and amputations. Depending on their impairment, cyclists at the Paralympic Games

Chinese medal prospect Qi Tang.

Key facts

Venue: Velodrome, London

Dates: 30 August – 2 September

Current Paralympic champions:

Men's Kilo: Anthony Kappes and Barney Storey (B&VI 1-3, Great Britain), Darren Kenny (CP3, Great Britain), Masashi Ishii (CP4, Japan), Mark Bristow (LC1, Great Britain), Jody Cundy (LC2, Great Britain), Simon Richardson (LC3-4, Great Britain)

Women's Kilo: Aileen McGlynn and Ellen Hunter (B&VI 1-3, Great Britain)

Men's Pursuit: Kieran Modra and Tyson Lawrence (B&VI 1-3, Australia), Darren Kenny (CP3, Great Britain), Christopher Scott (CP4, Australia), Michael Gallagher (LC1, Australia), Jiri Jezek (LC2, Czech Republic), Simon Richardson (LC3, Great Britain), Paolo Vigano (LC4, Italy)

Women's Pursuit: Aileen McGlynn and Ellen Hunter (B&VI 1-3, Great Britain), Sarah Storey (LC1-2/CP4, Great Britain), Barbara Buchan (LC3-4/CP3, USA)

Women's 500m: Jennifer Schuble (LC1-2/CP4, USA), Paula Tesoriero (LC3-4/CP3, New Zealand)

Men's Sprint: Anthony Kappes and Barney Storey (B&VI 1-3, Great Britain)

Team Sprint: Great Britain (LC1-4 CP3/4)

Star athlete: Darren Kenny

Born: 17/03/1970

Country: Great Britain

Events: Pursuit – C3, Kilo – C1/C2/C3, Team Sprint – C1-C5

Classification Category: C3

Paralympic Medals: Gold 1km Time Trial – CP3/4 and Individual Pursuit – CP3, Silver Combined Road Race and Time Trial – CP3 (Athens 2004); Gold 1km Time Trial – CP3, Team Sprint – LC1-4 CP3/4, Individual Pursuit – CP3 and Road Race – LC3-4/CP3, Silver Time Trial – CP3 (Beijing 2008)

Darren Kenny was a junior road racer of some repute when a neck injury towards the end of his teenage years appeared to have ended his career. After almost a decade away from the sport, Kenny returned at the age of 30 with the primary objective of improving his fitness.

He was soon invited to train with the Great Britain Paralympic Games squad and his talent was such that he was included in the team for Athens 2004.

Kenny returned with two golds and a silver and at Beijing 2008 he won four gold medals and one silver, shattering his own Individual Pursuit world record by more than five seconds during the preliminary round.

use either bicycles, tandems, handcycles or tricycles, although only the first two are involved in the Track programme.

Last year's World Track Championships in Italy did nothing to diminish the suggestion that Great Britain will once again be the nation to beat at London 2012. They won nine gold medals, including three more for Kenny, two for Sarah Storey and two – plus a silver – for Jody Cundy. Such

a period of dominance has ensured that the success of other countries has been marginalised. Australia and the USA apart, the only other nations to win gold on the track in Beijing were the Czech Republic, Italy, Japan and New Zealand. However, that is not to say that the medals will not be fiercely contested this time around. In total, 14 nations made it on to the podium in Beijing, and the Chinese haul of six medals, though none gold, also marked their emergence as a power in the sport.

Dong Jingping was among their star performers after claiming two bronze medals, in the women's 500m Time Trial (LC1-2/CP4) and also in the women's Individual Pursuit (LC1-2/CP4). Her countrywoman Qi Tang is likely to be the one to watch this time around in the 500m – C1/C2/C3 event,

having won gold at last year's World Championships.

The sport is now widely acknowledged to be one of the most popular of all those at the Paralympic Games, meaning that there is sure to be an electric atmosphere inside the 6,000-capacity Velodrome.

Ones to watch

1. **Jody Cundy** (Kilo – C4/C5, Great Britain)
2. **Qi Tang** (500m – C1/C2/C3, China)
3. **Aileen McGlynn and Ellen Hunter** (women's Kilo – B and women's Pursuit – B, Great Britain)

Classification categories

- **B** – Athletes who are blind or visually impaired and compete on a tandem with a sighted pilot on the front seat
- **C** – Athletes with cerebral palsy, limb impairments and amputations who compete on a bicycle. Each competitor is also given a class number – the lower the athlete's number, the greater the impact of their impairment on their ability to cycle

Cycling
Road

Brands Hatch may be better known as a motor sport circuit but the roaring engines will be replaced by pedal power when the venue plays host to the Road Cycling events this year.

Formula One Grand Prix races were held at Brands Hatch between 1964 and 1986 and all eyes will be on the Kent track again as the world's top Paralympic Games cyclists do battle for a place on the podium. The Road Races, Time Trials and Team Relay will all start and finish on the circuit's famous home straight, with part of the route also taking in local roads.

The impressive spectator facilities already in place should ensure large capacity crowds for events that have always captured the imagination within the Paralympic Games programme since they were first included at Stoke Mandeville and New York in 1984. And there will also be a sense of the sport coming home, as Brands Hatch owes its origins to the cycle tracks that criss-crossed the area in the 1920s.

While Track Cycling is a relatively new addition to the Paralympic Games competition

Sarah Storey will be aiming to add to her World Championships gold in the Time Trial.

Key facts

Venue: Brands Hatch, Kent

Dates: 5-8 September

Current Paralympic champions:

Men's Road Race: Andrzej Zajac and Dariusz Flak (B&VI 1-3, Poland), Heinz Frei (HC B, Switzerland), Ernst van Dyk (HC C, South Africa), Fabio Triboli (LC1-2/CP4, Italy), Darren Kenny (LC3-4/CP3, Great Britain),

Women's Road Race: Iryna Fiadotava and Alena Drazdova (B&VI 1-3, Belarus), Andrea Eskau (HC A/B/C, Germany)

Mixed Road Race: David Stone (CP1-2, Great Britain)

Men's Time Trial: Christian Venge, David Llaurado (B&VI 1-3, Spain),

Javier Otxoa (CP3, Spain), Cesar Neira (CP4, Spain), Wolfgang Schattauer (HC A, Austria), Heinz Frei (HC B, Switzerland), Oz Sanchez (HC C, USA), Wolfgang Sacher (LC1, Germany), Jiri Jezek (LC2, Czech Republic), Laurent Thirionet (LC3, France), Michael Teuber (LC4, Germany), Barbara Buchan (LC3-4/CP3, USA)

Women's Time Trial: Karissa Whitsell, Mackenzie Woodring (B&VI 1-3, USA), Rachel Morris (HC A/B/C, Great Britain), Sarah Storey (LC1-2/CP4, Great Britain)

Mixed Time Trial: David Stone (CP1-2, Great Britain)

Team Relay H1-H4: N/A

Classification categories

- **B** – Athletes who are blind or visually impaired and compete on a tandem with a sighted pilot on the front seat
- **C** – Athletes with cerebral palsy, limb impairments and amputations who compete on a bicycle
- **H** – Athletes with impairments that affect their legs and who compete using handcycles
- **T** – Athletes whose balance would make them unable to ride a bicycle and so compete using tricycles

With the exception of B Category, each competitor is given a class number – The lower the athlete's class number, the greater the impact of their impairment on their ability to cycle

programme, Road Cycling has long been firmly established as one of the blue-riband showpieces. The discipline has come a long way since its introduction, when it consisted of tandem classes for visually impaired riders, who competed along with a non-disabled pilot.

Six medal events were contested on its Games debut, only one of which was for women, but the programme will be much bigger at London 2012, thanks largely to significant technological developments. Alongside the tandems, athletes will also compete using handcyles and tricycles, and there will be 32 events on this year's Road Cycling competition programme.

Handcycles have two wheels at the rear and one at the front and require immense upper-body strength to generate speed.

Athletes who are unable to race on a two-wheeled bicycle because of their impairment use a tricycle.

Road Races see a mass start, where competitors line up together and the first across the line takes gold, while Time Trials require athletes to start at staggered intervals and attempt to clock the fastest time over the course. In addition, a Team Relay event is run in the H1-H4 handcycling class.

Hosts Great Britain may have won more than half the gold

Ones to watch

1. **Sarah Storey** (women's Time Trial – C5, Great Britain)

2. **Heinz Frei** (men's Road Race – H2, Switzerland)

3. **Aitor Oroza Flores** (mixed Road Race – T1/T2, Spain)

medals on offer in the Track Cycling events at Beijing 2008, but the Road Cycling competition was a different story. While Team GB won only two golds, it was Spain who dominated, topping the medal count in the men's events with three golds, two silvers and a bronze in the Time Trials, along with a Road Race silver. Switzerland, the United States and Germany also claimed multiple victories and will be expecting more success this time around.

However, the Para-Cycling Road World Championships in Roskilde, Denmark in 2011 did provide some cause for optimism for the hosts.

A Time Trial success for Sarah Storey on that occasion suggests that Great Britain will at least have one strong contender to capture a gold medal in the women's competition.

Control and discipline will be needed in abundance by riders competing in the Championships Test: Individual events, who will aim to deliver the perfect routines that will earn them a place at the top of the podium.

Equestrian is one of the most inclusive sports on show at London 2012 and is designed to allow riders with a broad range of impairments to compete against each other on equal terms.

Men and women go head-to-head against each other, with riders classified into five grades according to their level of impairment and the movements they can perform. Grade Ia riders have an impairment with the greatest impact on their ability to ride, while Grade IV riders have impairments that have the least impact on their overall performance.

The competition involves completing a set routine, which all riders must perform around an arena that is either 40 x 20 metres or 60 x 20m in size, depending on the grade in which they compete.

The routine consists of a variety of different tests, with the judges scoring a rider's performance in each discipline. Competitors are also judged on their overall control of the horse, their pace and also their skill in the saddle. The total marks are combined together to give a percentage, with the highest overall score taking the gold medal.

However, in order to ensure fairness right across the competition, the same routines are not performed in each grade. Tests for Grade Ia, Grade Ib and Grade II riders involve only the walk and trot movements, while riders in Grade III and IV perform a series of more varied tests, such as a canter – a steady, controlled gait in which three of the horse's legs must be off the ground at the same time.

In most Paralympic Games sports, the athlete is only responsible for their own performance, but Equestrian riders need to ensure that their horse achieves the highest level as well, meaning that communication between the two is fundamental to completing a good routine.

Depending on their level of impairment, riders are permitted

Key facts

Venue: Greenwich Park, London

Dates: 1-2 September

Current Paralympic champions:
Championships Test: Individual Ia
– Anne Dunham (Great Britain)
Championships Test: Individual Ib
– Lee Pearson (Great Britain)
Championships Test: Individual II
– Britta Napel (Germany)
Championships Test: Individual III
– Hannelore Brenner (Germany)
Championships Test: Individual IV
– Philippa Johnson (S. Africa)

Ones to watch

1. **Lee Pearson** (Championships Test: Individual – Grade Ib, Great Britain)

2. **Anne Dunham** (Championships Test: Individual – Grade Ia, Great Britain)

3. **Britta Napel** (Championships Test: Individual – Grade II, Germany)

German rider Bettina Eistel rides Fabuleux 5 on her way to bronze at Beijing 2008.

Star athlete: Sophie Christiansen

Born: 14/11/1987

Country: Great Britain

Events: Championships Test: Individual and Team – Open; Freestyle Test: Individual

Classification: Ia, Team – Open

Paralympic Medals: Bronze Championships Test: Individual – Grade I (Athens 2004); Gold Freestyle Test: Individual – Grade Ia and Team – Open, Silver Championships Test: Individual – Grade Ia (Beijing 2008)

Sophie Christiansen has developed into one of the world's top Equestrian riders. At 16 she was the youngest member of the Great Britain squad at Athens 2004, where she took bronze in the Championships Test: Individual – Grade I competition.

Christiansen continued her rise with Freestyle Test: Individual gold in the World Championships in 2007 and bronze in the Championships Test: Individual, before more Paralympic Games glory at Beijing 2008 when she won gold in the Freestyle Test: Individual, silver in the Championships Test: Individual and was part of the Great Britain quartet that won Team – Open gold.

Classification categories

- Athletes are classified across five grades, with Grade Ia for athletes whose impairment has the greatest impact on their ability to ride, through to Grade IV for athletes whose impairment has the least impact on their ability to ride

2004 prior to his exploits in the Chinese capital.

He will once again be the one to look out for on home soil at London 2012 and with a passionate British crowd cheering him on, he is likely to be a major medal contender

British riders have dominated recent Equestrian events, and Anne Dunham (Grade Ia) and Sophie Wells (Grade IV) are also expected to challenge for medals.

The hosts will face stiff competition from the likes of Norway, Denmark and Germany, with the latter a particularly strong team having taken the gold medal through Britta Napel in the Championships Test: Individual – Grade II event at Beijing 2008.

Equestrian has grown steadily over the last 25 years, having first appeared at the Stoke Mandeville and New York 1984 Games and featured at every Games since Atlanta 1996. That progress will continue at London 2012, where the competition will take place at the picturesque Greenwich Park, the oldest Royal Park in London.

There will be five gold medals up for grabs in total in the Championships Test: Individual events, setting the scene for what is sure to be another compelling competition.

to use aids, such as dressage crops or connecting rein bars, to help control their horse. Visually impaired athletes can also use 'callers' to guide them around the arena. At Sydney 2000, Norway's Anne Cecilie Ore, who is completely blind, rode her horse to the sound of a whistle and went on to win two silver medals.

Riders are scrutinised by the judges on every aspect of their performance, even their ability to use their aids, meaning that Equestrian is an extremely tough sport to master.

Top riders spend long periods of time training their animal to build up the kind of rapport that is required to produce the very best routines. For example, Great Britain's Lee Pearson – the most decorated Equestrian rider in Paralympic Games history – trained on his horse, Gentleman, for eight months before going on to win three gold medals at the Beijing 2008 Games.

Pearson has won nine gold medals and has dominated the Grade Ib Equestrian events for many years, also winning the title at Sydney 2000 and Athens

Equestrian
Freestyle Test: Individual and Team – Open

The Freestyle Test: Individual and Team – Open events are likely to see some fierce competition for medals, with the host nation in particular expected to mount a strong challenge to continue their success in the sport.

Equestrian events were first developed in the 1970s, with the very first competitions being held in Great Britain and Scandinavia. The 1984 Games in New York and Stoke Mandeville saw it introduced for the first time at the Paralympic Games, and a steady increase in its popularity means that it is now practised in over 40 countries worldwide.

Many of the leading nations will be represented at London 2012, with five Freestyle Test: Individual gold medals up for grabs, as well as the prestigious Team – Open title.

Whereas in the Championships Test: Individual event competitors are given a set series of moves to perform, the Freestyle Test:

Individual competition allows riders to inject more flair and personality into their routine. There are some compulsory requirements that must be completed, but athletes can also incorporate their own elements and, in addition, they choose the music they perform to in order to create a unique routine.

The competition takes place in an arena that is 40 x 20 metres, but events for the Grade IV riders can be in a slightly larger 60 x 20m area. Markers in the form of letters are placed around the competition venue and set moves are then performed in letter sequence. For example, the 'HEK Medium Walk' would see the rider and horse start their routine at the letter H, go past

E and then K demonstrating a medium walk. Riders are scored by the judges on their ability to control the horse and the skill with which they perform the moves in their routine. Once the scores are added up, each rider is given an overall percentage and the rider with the highest figure wins.

The judges at London 2012 will be looking for harmony and communication between the rider and their horse, and the relationship that is established between the two is important when it comes to challenging for medals, especially as success or failure can come down to the smallest of margins.

Musicality plays a particularly important part in the Freestyle

Key facts

Venue: Greenwich Park, London

Dates: 30 August – 4 September

Current Paralympic champions:

Freestyle Test: Individual Ia – Sophie Christiansen (Great Britain)

Freestyle Test: Individual Ib – Lee Pearson (Great Britain)

Freestyle Test: Individual II – Lauren Barwick (Canada)

Freestyle Test: Individual III – Hannelore Brenner (Germany)

Freestyle Test: Individual IV – Philippa Johnson (Canada)

Team – Open: Great Britain

Germany's Angelika Trabert rides Londria 2 in the Freestyle Test: Individual – Grade II in Beijing.

Classification categories

- Athletes are classified across five grades, with Grade Ia for athletes whose impairment has the greatest impact on their ability to ride, through to Grade IV for athletes whose impairment has the least impact on their ability to ride

Ones to watch

1. **Lee Pearson** (Freestyle Test: Individual – Grade Ib, Great Britain)

2. **Hannelore Brenner** (Freestyle Test: Individual – Grade III, Germany)

3. **Angelika Trabert** (Freestyle Test: Individual – Grade II, Germany)

Test: Individual event, with the music chosen by the rider often being used as a means of emphasising and enhancing the pace of the horse.

The keenly-anticipated Team – Open competition adds another dimension to the Equestrian events, as the best three or four members from each country are brought together to battle it out for the title. Riders from any grade are allowed to compete, although there must be at least one Grade I or Grade II athlete on each team.

In the Team – Open competition, each rider completes a set routine and their scores are combined with their performance in the Championships Test: Individual event to give an overall rating. Each team's final ranking is based on the sum of their best three performers in the Team – Open competition and the

Star team: Great Britain

Event: Team – Open

Paralympic Medals: Gold (Atlanta 1996), Gold (Sydney 2000), Gold (Athens 2004), Gold (Beijing 2008)

When it comes to the Team – Open competition, Great Britain have been untouchable, having won gold at each Games since the event's debut at Atlanta 1996.

In Lee Pearson (above, left) they have Equestrian's most successful-ever athlete (see feature on page 100), while team-mate Anne

Dunham has been one of the most consistent performers in the sport's history. She has been part of every successful Great Britain team and is likely to play a leading role once again at London 2012.

However, competition for a place in the line-up for the 2012 team looks set to be fierce, with the likes of Sophie Christiansen, Emma Sheardown, Sophie Wells and Ricky Balshaw all having produced fine performances at the 2010 World Championships.

Championships Test: Individual events, with the highest overall collated team score winning gold. In those teams with four riders, the lowest individual's score is excluded.

Equestrian will be one of the major sports being targeted for medals by the hosts at London 2012, with Great Britain having emerged as the dominant force in the team competition in particular over recent years.

Britain have won gold at every Paralympic Games since the event was first introduced to the programme at Atlanta 1996.

They will be led by the most successful rider in Equestrian history, Lee Pearson, and will be the favourites to once

again triumph on home soil in Greenwich Park.

There is also likely to be a strong challenge from some of the other leading European nations. In particular, big things are again expected of Germany, who claimed the silver medal at the Beijing 2008 Games, where they were led by their double Paralympic Games champion Hannelore Brenner.

Brenner claimed gold medals in the Championships Test: Individual – Grade III event and also in the Freestyle Test: Individual – Grade III event aboard her horse Women Of The World, and she has been widely tipped to defend her titles four years on.

Football
5-a-side and 7-a-side

The Football competitions are certain to excite the crowds as Brazil bid to win a third consecutive 5-a-side gold medal and the Ukraine aim to complete a hat-trick of their own in the 7-a-side competition.

Ones to watch

1. **Iran** (Football 7-a-side)
2. **Brazil** (Football 5-a-side)
3. **Russia** (Football 7-a-side)

Football is one of the highlights of the Games competition programme and is sure to attract plenty of interest. The 5-a-side competition is played by visually impaired athletes with a ball that has a bell contained inside it. Each team consists of four outfield players with a B1 visual impairment, while the goalkeeper can be sighted or have a lesser visual impairment.

In order to ensure fairness of competition, outfield players wear blackout masks as they seek to score more goals than the other team in a match that consists of two 25-minute halves. If the scores are level at the end of the 50 minutes, 10 minutes extra time is played. If scores are still level at the end of that period, the game is decided by a penalty shootout.

Each team is allowed a guide behind the opponents' goal to help direct the players, while the coach acts as a guide in the middle of the pitch and the goalkeeper also guides the players in the defensive third.

With no throw-ins and a rebound wall surrounding the pitch, 5-a-side Football is fast-paced and players require a high level of stamina as well as skill. There will be eight men's teams in the tournament

Spain take on China in the 5-a-side Football competition at Bejing 2008.

Star team: Ukraine

Event: Football 7-a-side

Paralympic Medals: Silver (Sydney 2000), Gold (Athens 2004), Gold (Beijing 2008)

Ukraine only began competing at the Paralympic Games in 1996 and four years later, at Sydney 2000, the 7-a-side Football team announced themselves on the global stage. Having won their group and beaten Brazil after extra time in the semi-finals, Ukraine faced their neighbours, Russia, in the final and suffered a narrow 3-2 defeat to take the silver medal.

However, they got their revenge at Athens 2004, as they defeated Russia 4-1 in the semi-finals before a victory over Brazil by the same scoreline in the final gave them gold.

Beijing 2008 saw old rivalries renewed with Russia and the two went head-to-head in the final. Inspirational captain Volodymyr Antonyuk scored twice in extra time as Ukraine retained their Paralympic Games title with a 2-1 win.

of the 7-a-side competition for disabled athletes on the international stage came at the 1978 CPISRA International Games in Edinburgh. It was not long before it was included at the Paralympic Games, and the sport made its debut at the Stoke Mandeville and New York 1984 Games, with Belgium taking the inaugural gold medal.

The Netherlands then went on to dominate 7-a-side Football, winning gold at Seoul 1988, Barcelona 1992 and Atlanta 1996. Russia took the title at Sydney 2000 but their neighbours, Ukraine, have emerged as a major force since then, having won gold at Athens 2004 and Beijing 2008. Ukraine and Russia are sure to be challengers once again at London 2012.

One of the success stories of the 7-a-side Football competition has been the emergence of the Iran team. In their debut at Athens 2004, they managed a creditable fifth-place finish and shocked many people by coming second at the World Championships in 2007. They suffered a 5-0 defeat to eventual silver medallists Russia in the semi-finals at Beijing 2008 but recovered in style to beat Brazil 4-0 to win the bronze, their first 7-a-side Football medal. They have since continued their development and defeated Paralympic Games champions Ukraine to take second place at the 2011 World Championships.

at London 2012, organised into two groups. The top two teams from each group go through to the semi-finals, with the winners fighting it out for the gold medal. Brazil are the best 5-a-side team in the world and have won gold at both Games since the sport was introduced at Athens 2004.

The 7-a-side Football tournament is contested by players who have problems walking and running but not when kicking the ball, and is sure to be another exciting spectacle. Players are classified at levels from C5 through to C8, with the C5 players having the greatest level of impairment. Each team must have at least one C5 or C6 player feature throughout the match and they

are allowed no more than three players from the C8 category on the pitch at any one time.

The game is played according to regular FIFA rules, except that the pitch and the goals are smaller, throw-ins must be taken using one hand and there is no offside rule. In 7-a-side competition, each half lasts 30 minutes and, should the scores be level after an hour, the game goes to a golden goal extra-time period of two 10-minute halves where the first team to score wins. As in the 5-a-side competition, if the scores are still level after extra time then the match goes to penalty kicks.

Football is widely regarded as the world's most popular sport and the introduction

Key facts

Venue: Riverbank Arena, London

Dates: 31 August – 9 September

Current Paralympic champions:
Football 5-a-side: Brazil
Football 7-a-side: Ukraine

Brazil are crowned kings of Football 5-a-side

Given their status as the most successful footballing nation of all time, Brazil's Paralympic Football stars have always had a tough act to follow – but they have more than lived up to expectations since the 5-a-side competition was first introduced to the schedule. The South Americans dominated the event on its debut at Athens 2004, beating Argentina 3-2. However, it was four years later, at Beijing 2008, that they really made the world sit up and take notice, beating hosts China 2-1 to cement their place as the undisputed kings of the sport.

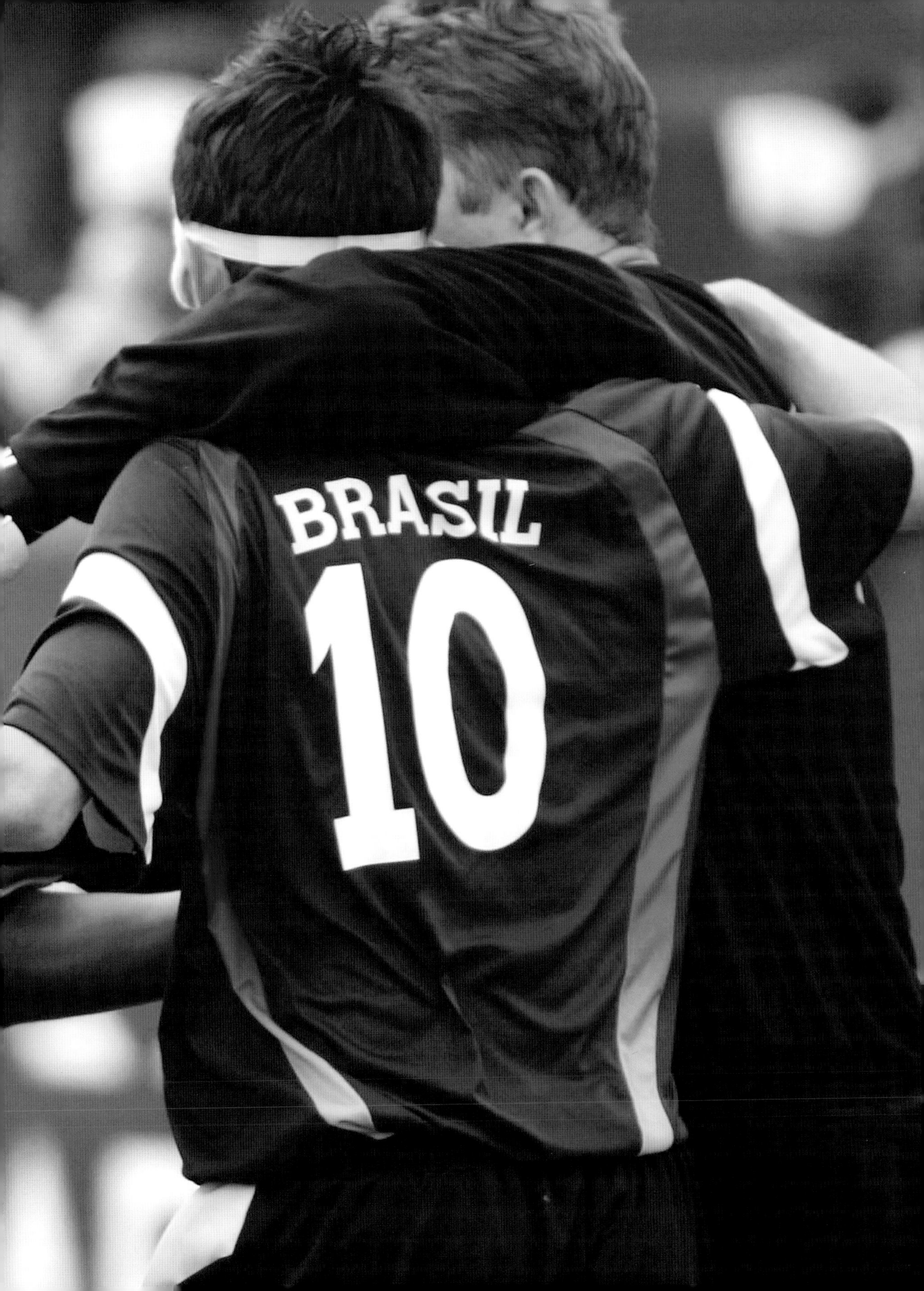
BRASIL
10

Goalball

There will be plenty of drama and excitement, but also total silence from the thousands of spectators inside the Copper Box, when the fast-paced sport of Goalball is played at the Games.

The sport is designed for blind or partially sighted athletes and is played with a ball that contains bells inside it, so the need for competitors to be able to hear where that ball is at all times is of paramount importance when the game is under way – although crowd participation and cheering is encouraged when a goal has been scored.

The aim of Goalball is for a team to roll the hard rubber ball into the goal of their opponents, who can attempt to block a shot using their bodies by standing in the team area in front of the goal. Teams comprise three players – two playing on the wings and one in the centre – and each member must wear eyeshades. This ensures that athletes with varying degrees of visual impairment can compete together on an equal basis.

The sport is played on an indoor court, with the lines of the court being tactile so that players know where they are in relation to the goal. The goal itself is nine metres wide and 1.3m high, while the court is 18 x 9m and is divided into three sections: a team area, a landing area and a neutral area in the middle separated by a centre line. There are three basic rules when it comes to throwing

the ball, which weighs 1.25 kilograms and has eight holes so that the noise of the bells can be heard clearly. When the ball is thrown it must touch the floor before passing over the centre line. Competitors must also throw within 10 seconds of gaining control of the ball, with passing also allowed in that time. The third rule is that no player can take more than two consecutive throws for their team.

Teams are penalised for breaking these rules and also for infractions such as throwing the ball before an official has called 'play', touching their eyeshades or defending a ball while out of the team area.

Each team takes it in turns to try to score, with the game split into two 12-minute halves. The only time there is a stoppage is

Key facts

Venue: Copper Box, London
Dates: 30 August – 7 September
Current Paralympic champions:
China (men's tournament), USA (women's tournament)

Players in a three-person Goalball team can only defend the ball when inside the team area in front of the goal.

after a goal has been scored or if the ball crosses a sideline.

If a game ends tied, two overtime periods of three minutes each are played and if the match is still level then free throws are taken.

Athletes need to have good speed and reflexes to shine in Goalball, which will be split into men's and women's competitions at London 2012. The 12 men's teams will be divided into two groups of six and the 10 women's teams are split into two pools of five. In both competitions, the top four teams in each group progress to the knockout stages. Goalball has three different classifications, from B1 to B3, which divide athletes based on their degree of visual impairment.

The sport was introduced in 1946 as an activity to help the rehabilitation of blind war veterans from the Second World War, and it was first seen at the Paralympic Games in Toronto in 1976, when it appeared as a demonstration sport. At the 1980 Games in Arnhem, Goalball was officially played as a medal event for the first time, while a women's competition was added in 1984.

Canada's women and Denmark's men's team have traditionally been powerhouses

Classification categories

- All athletes must meet a minimum standard of visual impairment

Ones to watch

1. **Lithuania** (men's tournament)
2. **China** (men's tournament)
3. **Canada** (women's tournament)

Star team: USA Women

Paralympic Medals: Gold (Stoke Mandeville and New York 1984), Silver (Seoul 1988), Bronze (Atlanta 1996), Silver (Athens 2004), Gold (Beijing 2008)

America's women reasserted themselves as the dominant force in women's Goalball at Beijing 2008, 24 years after their last Paralympic Games title.

Asya Miller (pictured) was their star player as they won gold in China, scoring all six goals in a 6-5 victory over the hosts and netting the winner with 49 seconds remaining.

That marked a return to the peak of the game for the USA, who claimed gold in the first women's event at Stoke Mandeville and New York 1984, before being forced to settle for silver twice, at Seoul 1988 and Athens 2004, and a bronze on home soil at Atlanta 1996.

in the sport, with both winning back-to-back Paralympic Games titles at Sydney 2000 and Athens 2004.

More recently, China has enjoyed great success since making their debut in the sport on this stage at Beijing 2008. China's men are the defending champions after they came from 6-2 down at half-time against Lithuania to win a thrilling gold medal match 9-8 four years ago, although the Lithuanians turned the tables to beat the Chinese in the 2010 World Championships in Sheffield. Marius Zibolis of Lithuania and Liangliang Chen of China will be among the star names to watch out for at London 2012 as the two big rivals prepare to lock horns once again.

China's women claimed the world title ahead of Paralympic Games champions USA in 2010

and they will be among the contenders to top the podium once again, along with Canada, who have the free-scoring Nancy Morin in their ranks.

Hosts Great Britain will be making their debut in Goalball at this level and their women's team looks to have the best chance of making an impact after winning the 2009 European Championships, with Anna Sharkey likely to be their key player.

At the Paralympic test event in December 2011, Great Britain's women came fifth, only losing 1-0 to world champions and eventual tournament winners China and 5-3 to defending Paralympic Games champions USA. That should boost their hopes of doing well at the Games, after failing to make an impact at the 2010 World Championships in Sheffield when finishing only 11th.

Judo

Judo athletes will need to display the perfect mix of attack and defence when they battle it out for medals at ExCeL in the only martial art to appear on the Paralympic Games competition programme.

Judo was modified from the martial art ju-jitsu by Dr Jigoro Kano in Japan in 1882.

The first international Paralympic Judo tournaments were held in 1987 before being introduced on this stage at the Seoul 1988 Games.

There are few differences between the sport competed in by non-disabled athletes and that seen at the Paralympic Games. The competition rules and the styles on show are the same, with the major modification being that the visually impaired athletes are allowed to make contact with their opponent before the start of the match to establish the hold.

Another difference is that the mats on which bouts take place all have different textures so an athlete, or 'judoka', is aware of where the different zones start and finish. The main mat is known as a 'tatami', measuring 10 x 10 metres, and this is surrounded by a one-metre danger area and an outer safety area. The uniform worn is called a 'judogi', which is made with a heavy cotton material that makes it easier for a judoka to grab their opponent's collar, sleeve, chest or trousers. The aim for each judoka is to use different techniques to overcome their opponent. An athlete needs to employ an effective strategy while having their resilience, strength, balance and dexterity put to the test during the course of a bout, where getting the right mix of aggression and control can be the difference between success and failure.

Contests last five minutes, although a match is over if a judoka scores a 10-point 'ippon', which involves throwing an opponent with speed and force onto their backs. If no ippon score is registered, the judoka with the greatest number of points after five minutes wins. Other ways of scoring include

Brazil's Antônio Tenório Silva (in blue) has won four consecutive Judo gold medals.

Key facts

Venue: ExCeL, London

Dates: 30 August – 1 September

Current Paralympic champions:

Men

Extra Lightweight (up to 60kg): Mouloud Noura (Algeria)

Half-Lightweight (60-66kg): Sidali Lamri (Algeria)

Lightweight (66-73kg): Eduardo Avila Sanchez (Mexico)

Half-Middleweight (73-81kg): Isao Cruz (Cuba)

Middleweight (81-90kg): Oleg Kretsul (Russia)

Half-Heavyweight (90-100kg): Antonio Tenorio Silva (Brazil)

Heavyweight (over 100kg): Ilham Zakiyev (Azerbaijan)

Women

Extra Lightweight (up to 48kg): Guo Huaping (China)

Half-Lightweight (48-52kg): Na Cui (China)

Lightweight (52-57kg): Lijing Wang (China)

Half-Middleweight (57-63kg): Naomi Soazo (Venezuela)

Middleweight (63-70kg): Carmen Herrera (Spain)

Heavyweight (over 70kg): Yanping Yuan (China)

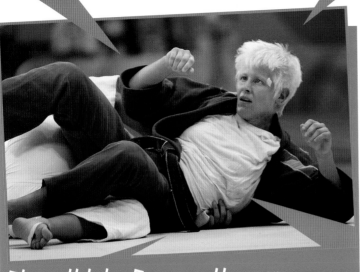

Star athlete: Carmen Herrera

Born: 26/09/1974

Country: Spain

Event: Women's Middleweight (63-70kg)

Classification Category: B3

Paralympic Medals: Gold women's Middleweight (63-70kg) (Athens 2004), Gold women's Middleweight (63-70kg) (Beijing 2008)

Carmen Herrera will be aiming for a third consecutive Paralympic Games Judo gold medal at London 2012. The Spanish judoka won the Women's Middleweight (63-70kg) title at Athens 2004, the first Games to include women's Judo, and retained her title at Beijing 2008.

The Malaga athlete, renowned for her attacking moves, suffered a knee injury that ended her hopes of challenging at the World Championships in 2010 but put that disappointment behind her to claim another top honour with gold at the IBSA World Games last year.

Classification categories

- All athletes must meet a minimum standard of visual impairment

Ones to watch

1. **Ben Quilter** (men's Extra Lightweight (up to 60kg), Great Britain)
2. **Yanping Yuan** (women's Heavyweight (over 70kg), China)
3. **Antônio Tenório Silva** (men's Half-Heavyweight (90-100kg), Brazil)

the lesser throws of 'waza-ari' and 'yuko', while grappling techniques on the mat can be used, including trying to immobilise an opponent for 25 seconds or gaining a submission with arm locks or strangle holds.

In the event of a tie, the bout is decided by a golden score period, where the first person to score a point wins. If after five minutes there are no further scores, the officials decide the outcome of the match.

In Judo competitions all athletes must meet a minimum standard of visual impairment.

Athletes are split into different weight categories for competition, with men contesting seven different medal events, from up to 60kg to over 100kg, while women have six weight categories, which range from up to 48kg to over 70kg.

At London 2012, the Judo events will be run in a knockout format, and athletes who have previously been beaten by either of the two finalists get to compete for one of two bronze medals in the repechage phase.

China led the standings at Beijing 2008 with seven medals, while Algeria, Brazil, Azerbaijan and Russia also had success. The Chinese will again have a strong squad and one of their big stars to watch out for is Yanping Yuan, the defending Paralympic Games and world champion in the women's Heavyweight (over 70kg) category. Brazil's Antônio Tenório Silva became the first athlete to win four consecutive gold medals in Judo with his victory in the men's Half-Heavyweight (90-100kg) class in 2008 and he will be going for a fifth straight title in London, although Gwang Geun Choi of South Korea has led the way in this category since Beijing after victory at the 2010 World Championships and the 2011 IBSA World Games.

Algeria's Sidali Lamri made a name for himself in 2008 when beating three-time Paralympic champion Satoshi Fujimoto of Japan in the Half-Lightweight final and he will be going for a second title, while fellow countryman Mouloud Noura will do battle with Great Britain's Ben Quilter at Extra Lightweight.

Quilter, who lost in the bronze medal match in Beijing, won the 2011 world title and is one of the medal hopefuls for the hosts, along with the likes of Samuel Ingram and Lesley Reid – who will look for inspiration to Simon Jackson, a three-time champion between 1988 and 1996.

Powerlifting

Athletes capable of lifting close to three times their own bodyweight will flex their muscles and show their strength in an attempt to be crowned Paralympic Games champion in the Powerlifting events.

Any disabled athlete can compete in the sport of Powerlifting, as long as they meet the minimum classification requirements for their particular impairment and they can extend their arms within 20 degrees of full extension during a lift. Competitors are grouped together based on their bodyweight, which means athletes with different impairments compete for the same medals. There are 10 different weight categories for men and women, with the men's weight classes going from Up to 48kg to Over 100kg and the women's ranging from Up to 40kg to Over 82.5kg.

Powerlifting is a bench-press competition that tests an athlete's upper-body strength. It is one of the fastest-growing sports at the Games, with more than 100 countries now participating on the international stage. With athletes constantly improving, world records are broken on a regular basis, and this is sure to make for an exciting spectacle for the crowd inside ExCeL at London 2012.

The sport sees a lifter lie completely flat on a 2.1-metre long bench that is no more than 50 centimetres off the ground, and a bar with weighted discs on it is lowered onto the competitors' extended arms. Athletes must then lower the bar to their chest, holding it motionless, before pressing it upwards to fully extend the arms and keep the elbows locked. Once the lift is completed, an immediate decision is given by three referees via a system of white and red lights as to whether the attempt has been successful or not.

Athletes have just two minutes to complete their lift from the time that their name is called and each competitor has three attempts in total, with a fourth being allowed if a lifter wishes

Chinese Taipei's Tzu Hui Lin celebrates gold in the women's Up to 75kg event at Beijing 2008.

Key facts

Venue: ExCeL, London

Dates: 30 August – 5 September

Current Paralympic champions:

Men

Up to 48kg: R.Ishaku (Nigeria)
Up to 52kg: G.Wu (China)
Up to 56kg: S.Othman (Egypt)
Up to 60kg: H.Mohammadi (Iran)
Up to 67.5kg: M.I.Mathna (Egypt)
Up to 75kg: L.Liu (China)
Up to 82.5kg: H.Zhang (China)
Up to 90kg: H.Cai (China)
Up to 100kg: D.Qi (China)

Over 100kg: K.Rajabigolojeh (Iran)

Women

Up to 40kg: L.Solovyova (Ukraine)
Up to 44kg: C.Xiao (China)
Up to 48kg: L.O.Ejike (Nigeria)
Up to 52kg: A.Perez (Mexico)
Up to 56kg: F.Omar (Egypt)
Up to 60kg: J.Bian (China)
Up to 67.5kg: T.Fu (China)
Up to 75kg: T.H.Lin (Chinese Taipei)
Up to 82.5kg: H.S.Ahmed (Egypt)
Over 82.5kg: R.Li (China)

Star athlete: Lidiya Solovyova

Born: 21/01/1978

Country: Ukraine

Event: Women's Up to 40kg

Classification Category: N/A

Paralympic Medals: Silver women's Up to 40kg (Sydney 2000), Gold women's Up to 40kg (Athens 2004), Gold women's Up to 40kg (Beijing 2008)

Lidiya Solovyova is one of the best female lifters in Paralympic Games history and will be looking to add to her long list of achievements at London 2012.

Having won silver in the women's Up to 40kg class at Sydney 2000, Solovyova then claimed gold at Athens 2004 and retained her title four years later in Beijing, beating her own world record in the process with a lift of 105.5kg.

The Ukrainian had to settle for silver at the 2010 World Championships, watching as Turkey's Nazmiye Muslu broke her record with a 106kg lift. However, she remains one of the leading lifters in the world and will look to go one better this time around.

67.5kg class, claiming gold for a third consecutive Paralympic Games. Yan Yang, who won the women's World Championship title in the Up to 56kg class in 2010, will look to lead the way for China this time around.

Egypt had 10 podium finishes in 2008 and reigning Paralympic Games champion Sherif Othman will once again be their big star to look out for in the men's Up to 56kg class.

Iran also have high hopes of bringing home more gold medals and, in Rahman Siamand, they have the athlete who has performed the largest weight lift in the history of the sport, following his 290kg world record at the 2010 Asian Para Games.

The defending champion in the men's Up to 60kg class, Iran's Hamzeh Mohammadi, will move up in weight to compete at 67.5kg this year, while Russia and Mexico also have a long list of athletes all with good chances of being among the medals, with Tamara Podpalnaya (women's Up to 52kg) and Amalia Pérez (women's Up to 60kg) among the leading contenders for their respective nations.

Classification categories

- Athletes must meet a minimum eligibility criteria based on their impairment

Ones to watch

1. **Amalia Pérez** (women's Up to 60kg, Mexico)
2. **Rahman Siamand** (men's Over 100kg, Iran)
3. **Yan Yang** (women's Up to 56kg, China)

to go for a record. After each round, the weight on the bar must increase by at least 2.5 kilograms and the overall winner is the athlete who ultimately lifts the largest weight.

Some of the reasons for a lift being declared unsuccessful by the referees include not fully extending the arms; not lifting the bar in a single, smooth movement; not holding the bar motionless to the chest; an athlete moving their position on the bench during the lift and an athlete not completing the lift in the set time.

Powerlifting made its debut at the Stoke Mandeville and New York 1984 Games, having previously been known as Weightlifting and only competed in by male athletes with spinal injuries. The sport has evolved a great deal and the competition is now open to all athletes with an impairment, with women competing for the first time at Sydney 2000. Around 200 athletes will take part across a total of 20 different medal events at this Games.

China will once again bring a strong squad of athletes, as they try to emulate the 14 medals they won on home soil at Beijing 2008, which included a haul of nine golds. Taoying Fu was their star lifter four years ago after winning the women's Up to

Rowing

Spectators at Eton Dorney can expect fierce competition in the sport of Rowing, which is the newest to be included on the Paralympic Games programme programme, having been introduced for the first time at Beijing 2008.

More commonly referred to as Adaptive Rowing, the sport dates back to the 1970s when it was first seen in Australia, Great Britain and Germany. During the 1990s, a number of exhibition events were held at the World Rowing Championships, but it was not until four years ago that Adaptive Rowing finally appeared on the Games stage.

Adaptive Rowing is open to athletes with physical and sensory impairments. The title 'Adaptive' means that the equipment is adapted for the rower, with three different boats used. Regardless of which type of boat is competed in, all rowers require immense upper-body strength, power, stamina and determination. Men and women compete together at the Games, except in the Single Sculls class, which is for athletes who only have movement in their arms and shoulders. These AS1x boats have a fixed seat that offers postural support to athletes who need it for their upper body so they stay in a fixed position. The boats have buoyancy devices, called pontoons, attached to the riggers to act as stabilisers and give extra lateral balance.

The Double Sculls – TAMix2x class is for athletes who only have movement in their arms and trunk and also uses boats with a fixed seat to add extra support. In competitions, one man and one woman row in the same boat and each use two oars to propel the boat. They compete in races over 1000m – the recognised race distance for all Adaptive Rowing events.

The Coxed Four LTAMix4+ event sees teams of four rowers and a cox compete using the sweeping technique, where athletes have one oar each. Athletes with movement in their arms, trunk and legs compete in this mixed-gender class, which is the only type of boat where athletes use a sliding seat. One constant is the hull of all the Paralympic Games boats, which is the same size as those used at the Olympic Games.

Great Britain have always excelled at Rowing and the host nation will hope to enjoy further success this year, especially as they won two of the four gold medals on offer at the Beijing 2008 Games thanks to victories

Classification categories

- **AS** – Athletes with movement in only their arms and shoulders. Men and women compete separately in Single Sculls events
- **TA** – Athletes with movement in only their trunk and arms. Men and women compete together in mixed Double Sculls events
- **LTA** – Athletes with movement in their legs, trunk and arms. Men and women compete together in mixed Coxed Four events

French medal contender Nathalie Benoit.

Key facts

Venue: Eton Dorney, Buckinghamshire

Dates: 31 August – 2 September

Current Paralympic champions:

Men's Single Sculls – ASM1x: Tom Aggar (Great Britain)

Women's Single Sculls – ASW1x: Helene Raynsford (Great Britain)

Double Sculls – TAMix2x: Yangjing Zhou and Zilong Shan (China)

Coxed Four – LTAMix4+: Paola Protopapa, Luca Agoletto, Daniele Signore, Graziana Saccocci and Alessandro Franzetti (Italy)

Star athlete: Tom Aggar

Born: 24/05/1984

Country: Great Britain

Event: Men's Single Sculls – ASM1x

Classification Category: AS

Paralympic Medals: Gold men's Single Sculls – ASM1x (Beijing 2008)

Tom Aggar has dominated the Single Sculls – ASM1x class since he started rowing competitively in 2007. In the British rower's first year of competition he became world champion and a year later he took gold at the Beijing 2008 Games.

Since his success in China, Aggar has gone on to win gold at the World Championships three consecutive times and now heads into London 2012 as a big favourite.

Aggar took up rowing as part of his rehabilitation from a spinal injury he suffered in 2005, which resulted in the paralysis of his legs.

After being named Adaptive Rower of the Year by the International Rowing Federation (FISA) in January 2010, Aggar defended his world title in style that year – winning gold by over 13 seconds.

for Tom Aggar and Helene Raynsford in the Single Sculls – AS1x events.

While Aggar is the dominant force in the men's event, after winning the last five major international titles on offer, Raynsford is aiming to retain her title having come out of retirement to compete at the beautiful setting of Eton Dorney in Buckinghamshire. However, she will face a tough task to win another gold as France's Nathalie Benoit – who triumphed at the 2010 World Championships – and Ukraine's Alla Lysenko – the 2009 and 2011 world champion – have led the way since the last Paralympic Games.

Great Britain also has high hopes of a medal in the Coxed Four – LTAMix4+ event after they won gold at the 2011 World Championships in Slovenia. Having been beaten by Canada to the line in the final in 2010, the British quartet regained the title they had won in 2009 with a great show of power in the second half of the race in Bled to turn the tables and edge out their big rivals.

Two-time world champions Iryna Kyrychenko and Dmytro Ivanov of Ukraine look to be the pair to watch out for in the Double Sculls – TAMix2x.

Ones to watch

1. **Nathalie Benoit** (women's Single Sculls – ASW1x, France)

2. **Iryna Kyrychenko and Dmytro Ivanov** (Double Sculls – TAMix2x, Ukraine)

3. **Canada** (Coxed Four – LTAMix4+)

The duo are highly-skilled and versatile athletes, with Ivanov having represented his country in the Javelin at the Paralympic Games and Kyrychenko having competed at the Winter Paralympic Games.

However, they will need to find their best form at London 2012 after the new Chinese pairing of Xiaoxian Lou and Tianming Fei won the World Championships title last year and left the Ukrainian pair out of the medals after they had led for much of the race.

All the Rowing events will start with heats, with two boats from each race qualifying directly for the final and all the remaining boats then competing in two repechage races to try to claim one of the remaining spots available in the final showdown for the medals.

Sailing

Mastering the full force of the wind and waves on the testing waters of Weymouth Bay on the south coast of England will be the challenge for the Sailing competitors at London 2012.

The sport requires a good knowledge of meteorology, a solid technique and an astute tactical brain to ensure that the right lines are taken around a course marked out by buoys. The need for a sailor to be able to hold their nerve as they race side-by-side with other boats in a fleet format is also key.

At the Paralympic Games, sailors can compete in classes with either one, two or three people in a boat at any one time, with men and women competing together. In each division, keelboats are used because the design of the boats provides greater stability and also an open cockpit to give the sailors more room. Slight modifications are allowed to the keelboats in order to suit an athlete's level of impairment – with the sport open to anyone with a physical or visual impairment. A classification system is used to ensure that there is a level playing field in each of the three events, the Single-Person Keelboat (2.4mR), the Two-Person Keelboat (SKUD18) and the Three-Person Keelboat (Sonar).

Paralympic Sailing employs a scoring system that assigns points to an athlete based on their level of impairment, which allows people from different disability groups to compete together. The higher the number the less the impact of the athlete's impairment on their ability to sail.

There are also rules governing the make-up of crews in boats where two or more sailors compete. Crews in the Two-Person Keelboat class need to include one female sailor and one sailor with a one-point classification, while the total

Sailors must hold their nerve as they compete at close quarters.

Classification categories

- **1-7** – The higher the number the less the impact of the athlete's impairment on their ability to sail. The combined total of crew points must not exceed 14 in a Three-Person Keelboat

- **TPA and TPB** – TPA athletes have an impairment that has a greater impact on their ability to sail than TPB athletes. A Two Person Keelboat's crew is made up of one TPA athlete and one TPB athlete

- **MD** – Athletes' impairment must meet minimum eligibility criteria to compete in the Single Person Keelboat

Star athlete: John Ruf

Born: 04/03/1968

Country: USA

Event: Single-Person Keelboat (2.4mR)

Classification Category: N/A

Paralympic Medals: Bronze Single-Person Keelboat (2.4mR) (Beijing 2008)

Having claimed bronze on his Paralympic Games debut at Beijing 2008, John Ruf will be hoping to reach the top of the podium this year. The talented American has split his time between working as an attorney in Wisconsin and training for the Games as he prepares to compete in the Single-Person Keelboat (2.4mR).

Ruf made a competitive introduction to the sport at the US Olympic trials in 2000 but it was not until eight years later that his big breakthrough came, at Beijing 2008.

the Paralympic Games crown in 2004 and took silver in 2008, although he could only manage seventh at the last World Championships, which were also held in Weymouth Bay.

Great Britain's medal hope in the Single-Person Keelboat is Helena Lucas and in the Two-Person Keelboat, three-time world champions Alexandra Rickham and Niki Birrell are expected to be in the hunt.

The defending Three-Person Keelboat champions from 2008 are Germany, although Israel will fancy their chances of coming out on top. Israel won gold at Athens 2004 and at the 2011 World Championships – led on both occasions by Dror Cohen, a former combat pilot with the Israeli Air Force who was paralysed from the waist down after being involved in a car accident in 1992.

points score for a crew in the Three-Person Keelboat event must not exceed 14, and at least one female sailor must be included. When assessing an athlete's impairment in order to give them a score, a classifier will judge their stability, hand function, mobility and vision.

Each class features up to 11 separate races and teams are given a score based on their finishing position (the better the placing the lower the score). The crew scoring the lowest number of points is declared the winner after the full race series.

At London 2012, Sailing will make only its fourth appearance at the Paralympic Games as a full medal event, with the Two-Person Keelboat being the newest of the events, having been introduced to the programme at the Beijing 2008 Games.

The origins of Sailing for athletes with an impairment go back to the 1980s. However, it was not until 1990 that Sailing was introduced as a demonstration event at the World Games for athletes with an impairment. The sport was first seen in the Paralympic Games at Atlanta 1996, where it was a successful exhibition event, after which it was added to the full programme at Sydney four years later.

This is, therefore, still a relatively new Paralympic Games sport and sailors will be heading into the London 2012 Games with an opportunity to begin writing their own chapter of history.

In the Single-Person Keelboat class, Thierry Schmitter of the Netherlands looks to be the one to beat after claiming the World Championships title in 2010 and retaining it in 2011, while Frenchman Damien Seguin won

Shooting
Pistol

There is very little margin for error in the pistol events within the Shooting competition, as the world's top marksmen and women aim to hit the centre of a target that is placed either 10, 25 or 50 metres away.

Having first featured at the Arnhem 1980 Games, the pistol events have grown into a regular feature of the Paralympic programme.

There are 12 events with seperate competitions for men and women in the 10m Air Pistol – SH1 category, while the 25m Pistol – SH1 and the 50m – SH1 competitions are mixed events. In each of these, success or failure comes down to a series of very fine margins, with even the grip of the gun moulded for an athlete's individual requirements in order to help them to shoot a competitive score.

Athletes with various physical disabilities compete against each other in the single SH1 class. This is then further divided into sub-classes of A, B and C, which are used to determined the level of back rest that an athlete is allowed on their shooting chair, depending on their impairment.

Pistol events see athletes fire a number of shots at a target, which has 10 concentric scoring values from one to 10. The goal is to fire as many shots as possible into the bullseye, which is worth a maximum 10 points. The permitted number of shots and the time allowed for athletes to complete these varies from event to event, but each competition has a qualification round followed by a final round. In the final round, the scoring rings are sub-divided further into additional zones, with the bullseye worth a maximum 10.9. Scores from the qualification round and final round are added to give an overall number of points, with the highest total claiming the gold medal.

Athletes competing in the 10m Air Pistol event use pistols with bullets that measure 4.5 millimetres in diameter, while those in the 25m and 50m events use .22 calibre pistols, which fire 5.6mm rounds. The targets are checked at the end of each series of shots, with judges counting the overall score for each athlete.

Russian shooters dominated the pistol competitions at the Beijing

Key facts

Venue: The Royal Artillery Barracks, London

Dates: 30 August – 6 September

Current Paralympic champions:

P1 – 10m Air Pistol – SH1: Valeriy Ponomarenko (Russia)

P2 – 10m Air Pistol – SH1: Lin Haiyan (China)

P3 – 25m Pistol – SH1: Andrey Lebedinskiy (Russia)

P4 – 50m Pistol – SH1: Park Sea-Kyun (South Korea)

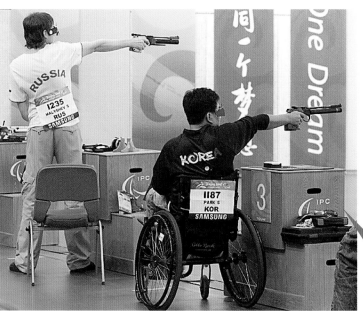

Russian and South Korean shooters in action at Beijing 2008, winning three out of four golds.

Star athlete: Valeriy Ponomarenko

Born: 19/08/1970

Country: Russia

Event: P1 – 10m Air Pistol – SH1

Classification: SH1

Paralympic Medals: Gold men's Air Pistol – SH1, Bronze mixed Sport Pistol – SH1 and mixed Free Pistol – SH1 (Beijing 2008)

Valeriy Ponomarenko produced the best performances of his career at Beijing 2008 and he will be looking to reach those heights once again in London.

The Russian made his first Paralympic Games appearance at Atlanta 1996 and came desperately close to winning a medal before finishing fourth in both the men's Air Pistol – SH1 and mixed Sport Pistol – SH1.

Twelve years later, in Beijing, Ponomarenko finally did earn a place on the podium and he did so in some style, taking bronze in both the mixed Free Pistol – SH1 and mixed Sport Pistol – SH1 before his crowning achievement came with gold in the men's Air Pistol – SH1. Ponomarenko broke the qualification and final world records on his way to becoming the Paralympic Games champion.

2008 Games, with Valeriy Ponomarenko winning gold in the P1 – 10m Air Pistol – SH1 event and also taking bronze in both the 25m and 50m events.

His team-mate, Andrey Lebedinskiy, also claimed a gold medal in the mixed Sport Pistol – SH1 class and the Russians look likely to be a force to be reckoned with once again at London 2012.

They are widely recognised as among the most technically-proficient Shooting nations, although the Chinese and South Koreans are also being tipped to be among the leading medal contenders, having also featured prominently four years ago.

Positioning is a key element of the technique required to compete at the highest level of the sport.

The exact position adopted by each athlete differs depending on their own individual style, but the rules state that competitors must shoot one-handed and that they are not allowed to have their non-shooting arm/hand on the shooting chair, if they use one.

Shooting events place incredible demands on competitors from both a mental and a physical perspective.

The outstretched arm used to hold and fire the pistol must be strong enough to control the weapon and maintain a consistently steady aim, with competition rounds usually consisting of 40 or in some cases 60 shots and lasting anything between 75 minutes and up to 120 minutes.

Pistol shooters tend to spend considerable time and effort working on building up their core strength. Good hand-eye co-ordination is also essential, and many top-level shooters can be seen wearing a headband and a blinder for one of their eyes in order to be able to focus as accurately as they possibly can on the target for long periods of time.

Classification categories

- **SH1** – Athletes who can support the weight of the firearm themselves

Ones to watch

1. **Andrey Lebedinskiy** (P3 – 25m Pistol – SH1, Russia)
2. **Park Sea-Kyun** (P4 – 50m Pistol – SH1, South Korea)
3. **Marina Klimenchenko** (P2 – 10m Air Pistol – SH1, Russia)

The rifle Shooting events are some of the most technical that will be on show at the London 2012 Games and, along with many other sports, competitors require years of practice and dedication to reach the very highest level.

Like many other sports, consistency is the key to good shooting, and in order to be among the leading contenders challenging for medals, the majority of shots will generally have to hit the highest-scoring 10-point centre ring.

Athletes are trained to make each shot almost identical so that they can consistently shoot high scores, and so meticulous attention to detail also comes into play. Every element in a shooter's routine, from the exact position they place their chair to the time it takes for them to take an individual shot, is perfected and practised time and time again to reduce the margin for error.

Trigger control is another critical element in separating the very best shooters from the field, as firing a shot a fraction of a second too early or marginally too late can mean the difference between a perfect 10 shot or hitting a lower score. Likewise, many top shooters

place great importance on their physical fitness as much as their mental conditioning, and the best rifle shooters also spend hours working on breathing techniques so that they can keep their focus during the tension of competition.

The most common positions seen in rifle Shooting are standing and prone. In standing events, SH1 athletes are able to shoot either standing or sitting, while SH2 athletes must be seated. In both cases, no elbow support is allowed. In the prone events, athletes shoot with both elbows resting on a shooting table.

The 50m Rifle 3 Positions event sees athletes fire an even number of shots in standing and prone positions, as well as in a kneeling position where one elbow rests on the table.

In total, there will be eight gold medals up for grabs in the rifle Shooting events at London 2012, which will be held at The Royal Artillery Barracks. Men and women will go head-to-head in two Air Rifle Prone events and one event for Air Rifle Standing, as well as the 50m Free Rifle Prone. The competition for medals in those mixed events will be fierce, while there are separate competitions for men and women in both the 10m Air Rifle Standing and the 50m Rifle 3

Swedish shooter Jonas Jacobsson is one of the most decorated male Paralympians.

Key facts

Venue: The Royal Artillery Barracks, London

Dates: 30 August – 6 September

Current Paralympic champions:

R1 – 10m Air Rifle Standing – SH1: Jonas Jacobsson (Sweden)

R2 – 10m Air Rifle Standing – SH1: Veronica Vadovicova (Slovakia)

R3 – 10m Air Rifle Prone – SH1: Matt Skelhon (Great Britain)

R4 – 10m Air Rifle Standing – SH2: Lee Ji-Seok (South Korea)

R5 – 10m Air Rifle Prone – SH2: Lee Ji-Seok (South Korea)

R6 – 50m Free Rifle Prone – SH1: Jonas Jacobsson (Sweden)

R7 – 50m Rifle 3 Positions – SH1: Jonas Jacobsson (Sweden)

R8 – 50m Rifle 3 Positions – SH1: Lee Yun-Ri (South Korea)

Star athlete: Matt Skelhon

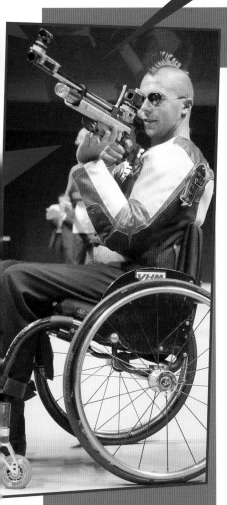

Born: 30/10/1984

Country: Great Britain

Event: R3 – 10m Air Rifle Prone – SH1

Classification: SH1

Paralympic Medals: Gold R3 – 10m Air Rifle Prone – SH1 (Beijing 2008)

The image of Matt Skelhon sporting a bright red mohawk celebrating his gold medal was one of the most distinctive of Beijing 2008.

Skelhon had only been training as a competitive rifle shooter for 18 months before he made his Paralympic Games debut in China.

It was widely expected that he would use that as an exercise to get experience, but few could have predicted what he would achieve in the R3 – 10m Air Rifle Prone – SH1 event, as he shot a perfect 600 from his 60 shots to equal the world record alongside Chinese shooter Zhang Cuiping in the qualification round.

Skelhon continued his inspired form in the final and held his nerve to defeat Zhang by half a point and take gold.

to support the rifle. SH2 athletes are also permitted to have a loader, who places ammunition into their gun before each shot.

Each classification has further sub-categories of A, B and C which dictate whether the athlete is allowed no back support, some back support or full back support on their shooting chair, depending on their impairment.

The rifle Shooting events have produced some amazing athletes down the years – but none more so than Sweden's Jonas Jacobsson, who is one of the most decorated male Paralympians of all time. Jacobsson has competed at eight consecutive Paralympic Games, from Arnhem 1980 to Beijing 2008, during which time he has won a phenomenal 16 gold, two silver and nine bronze medals, and he is expected to once again play a leading role.

Classification categories

- **SH1** – Athletes who can support the weight of the firearm themselves
- **SH2** – Athletes who have no ability to support the weight of the firearm with their arms and require a shooting stand

Ones to watch

1. **Jonas Jacobsson** (R1 – 10m Air Rifle Standing – SH1, R6 – 50m Free Rifle Prone – SH1, R7 – 50m Rifle 3 Positions – SH1, Sweden)
2. **Lee Ji-Seok** (R4 – 10m Air Rifle Standing – SH2, R5 – 10m Air Rifle Prone – SH2, South Korea)
3. **Zhang Cuiping** (R2 – 10m Air Rifle Standing – SH1, R3 – 10m Air Rifle Prone – SH1, China)

Positions – the latter of which requires plenty of versatility.

While medal-winning technique takes years to perfect, the goal of shooting is simple – with competitors aiming to fire the maximum number of their permitted shots as close to the centre of the target as possible.

Targets are made up of 10 concentric scoring rings, each with a numerical value. The centre ring, or bullseye, is worth a maximum 10 points, with the value of each ring decreasing down to the outside ring, which is worth one.

Each competition has a qualification round and the eight athletes with the highest

scores from that progress to the final, where they each fire a set number of individual timed shots on command.

The scoring in the final is enhanced, with the centre ring divided further so that a direct bullseye hit is worth 10.9 points. Scores are carried over from the qualification round, and the athlete with the highest combined score from qualification and the final takes the gold medal.

In Shooting, athletes are classified into either the SH1 or SH2 categories. SH1 athletes are able to support the weight of the rifle themselves, while SH2 athletes require a shooting stand

Sitting Volleyball

The world's best teams will battle it out for the gold medal across 10 days of action-packed competition as the Sitting Volleyball tournaments for the both men and women take place at ExCeL.

When Volleyball was first introduced to the Paralympic Games in 1976 it was originally a standing event, and it was only in Arnhem in 1980 that the sitting format of the game was incorporated into the competition programme. Initially, the two disciplines were staged together before the standing version was dropped after Sydney 2000.

Sitting Volleyball has since provided some of the most thrilling action of recent Games, although the sport actually dates back to the 1950s in the Netherlands, where it was invented using a combination of volleyball and a German game called sitzbal. As the founders of the sport, the Dutch claimed the gold medal on its Games debut in 1980 and again at the Stoke Mandeville and New York showpiece in 1984, but they were the losing finalists to Iran at each of the next two Games. The Middle Eastern nation have since gone on to cement their place as the dominant force in the men's competition, having won five Paralympic Games titles, including beating Bosnia and Herzegovina to reclaim their crown at Beijing 2008.

Iran and Bosnia are the two big powerhouses of the men's game, and they are widely expected to lead the way in the hunt for gold once again at London 2012, with the likes of Egypt, Russia and Brazil also expected to be in contention for medals. China, meanwhile, have won both women's tournaments at the Paralympic Games since 2004 and as the reigning world champions, they will be the team to beat once again.

The game shares many similarities with its non-disabled alternative, although it is played on a smaller indoor court, which measures 10 x 6 metres. The object for the two teams is to land the ball in the opponents' half of the court so that it is impossible to return. Each team is allowed three attacking touches of the ball before it must cross back over the net, which is 1.15m high for men

The 'block' at the net is one of the key features of Sitting Volleyball action.

Key facts

Venue: ExCeL, London
Dates: 30 August – 8 September
Current Paralympic champions: Iran (men's tournament), China (women's tournament)

Classification categories

- **D** – Athletes whose impairment has a greater impact on the field of play
- **MD** – Athletes whose impairment has a lesser impact on the field of play
- Of the six players on court, a maximum of one can be MD and of the 12 players on a team, a maximum of two can be MD

Star team: China Women

Paralympic Medals: Gold (Athens 2004), Gold (Beijing 2008)

China has dominated women's Sitting Volleyball since the sport was added to the Paralympic Games competition programme at Athens 2004.

Led by talented spiker Yuhong Sheng, they claimed the gold medal in both 2004 and again on home soil at Beijing 2008, beating the USA in a thrilling final four years ago. At the age of 39, Sheng inspired the Chinese to another victory over the Americans as they won the 2010 WOVD World Sitting Volleyball Championships, and the Asian nation have since continued to go from strength to strength.

They will be aiming for their third consecutive gold at London 2012.

Ones to watch

1. **Iran** (men's tournament)
2. **Bosnia and Herzegovina** (men's tournament)
3. **USA** (women's tournament)

and 1.05m high for women. Because the sport is played in a sitting position, part of an athlete's body between the buttocks and the shoulders must be in contact with the court when a player touches the ball. Over the course of the Games, fans will encounter a raft of Sitting Volleyball jargon, most commonly when the players 'block' the ball by creating a barrier with their hands at the net, or when attempting a 'dig' – a defensive shot from close to the ground. The 'set' is the act of setting the ball for a team-mate to attack at the net, usually on the second of a team's three permitted touches, while a 'wipe' sees a player return the ball off an opposing block so that it lands out of bounds.

Games are played over a best-of-five-set format, with the first team to reach 25 points by a clear two-point margin winning the set. If the match is tied at 2-2 in sets, then the fifth set is played until a team reaches 15 points, again by a margin of two. Six players from each team are allowed on the court at any one time, including a team leader and a specialist defensive player called the libero, who wears a different coloured uniform and cannot spike or serve the ball, but plays a key role.

Any athlete with a physical impairment can compete in Sitting Volleyball, although a classification system is used to determine the extent of a player's impairment. There are two main classification categories, D for athletes whose impairment has more impact on competition and MD for those for whom it has a lesser impact.

In this fast-paced game, competitors need particularly high levels of strength and agility, with players using their hands to manoeuvre their way around the court. Good balance and teamwork are also crucial to success.

At London 2012 there will be 10 men's teams and eight women's teams battling for the medals at ExCeL.

In both competitions, the tournament will begin with a round-robin group stage, with the top four men's teams in each group progressing to the quarter-finals and the top two women's teams in each group making it through to the semi-finals.

From there, the competition is played as a straight knockout event, with the final two teams going head-to-head for the gold medal.

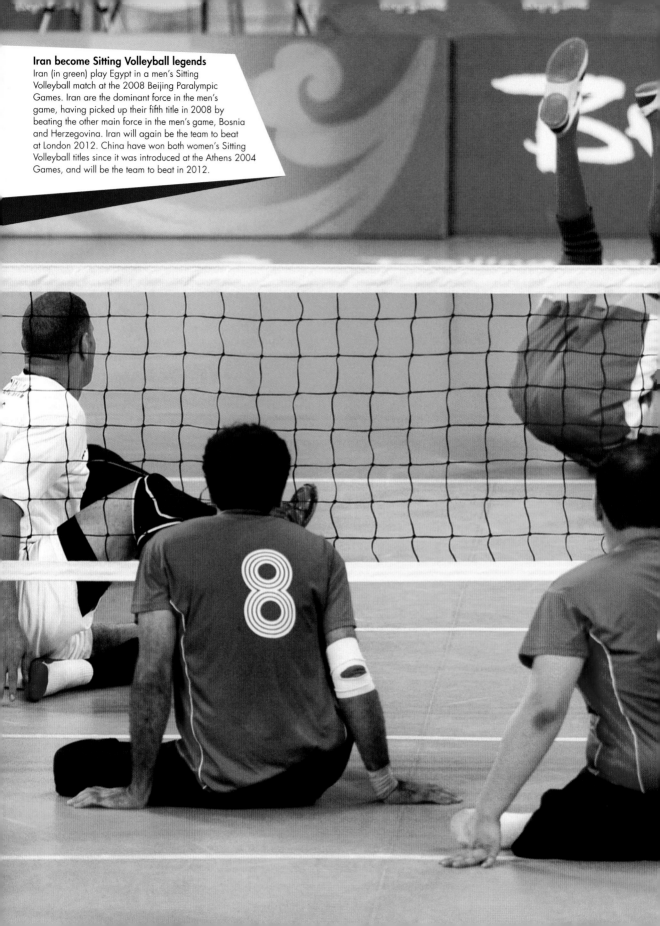

Iran become Sitting Volleyball legends

Iran (in green) play Egypt in a men's Sitting Volleyball match at the 2008 Beijing Paralympic Games. Iran are the dominant force in the men's game, having picked up their fifth title in 2008 by beating the other main force in the men's game, Bosnia and Herzegovina. Iran will again be the team to beat at London 2012. China have won both women's Sitting Volleyball titles since it was introduced at the Athens 2004 Games, and will be the team to beat in 2012.

Swimming
Breaststroke, Backstroke and Butterfly

Requiring superb technique and high levels of athleticism, the Breaststroke, Backstroke and Butterfly Swimming events are likely to witness some particularly fierce competition for medals.

Swimming is one of the most popular sports at the Games and thousands of spectators are expected to watch up to 600 swimmers from around 80 nations compete in the impressive surroundings of the Aquatics Centre, where a series of qualifying heats will determine the eight swimmers who progress to each final.

A total of 61 gold medals will be up for grabs across the three strokes, with Breaststroke, Butterfly and Backstroke races held over 50m and 100m. The only exceptions will be that women do not swim the 50m Breaststroke, while not every classification category competes in each event. To determine the classification categories, athletes are assessed on their

level of physical, visual or intellectual impairment, with a point score allocated to each swimmer based on their ability to perform each stroke. The intellectual impairment group, Class 14, makes a return to the programme at London 2012 after being absent at Athens 2004 and Beijing 2008. Class

Canadian Stephanie Dixon has 19 medals.

11-13 is likely to see some of the most keenly-contested events. This category is for athletes with varying levels of visual impairment, with all swimmers required to wear blackened goggles to ensure equality of competition. In these races, swimmers are allowed to have helpers, called 'tappers', who stand at the end of the pool and use a pole to tap a swimmer when they are approaching the wall to indicate when they should turn or when to finish.

In some circumstances, a swimmer's classification may vary depending on the effect their impairment has on the event in which they are competing. Breaststroke, for example, uses a greater leg kick, so an athlete with a particular

Key facts

Venue: Aquatics Centre, London

Dates: 30 August – 8 September

Current Paralympic champions:

Men's 50m Backstroke: C.Tampaxis (S1, Greece), D.Kokarev (S2, Russia), J.Du (S3, China), J.Reyes (S4, Mexico), D.Dias (S5, Brazil)

Women's 50m Backstroke: G.Ielisavetska (S2, Ukraine), P.Xiu Yip (S3, Singapore), B.Hlavackova (S5, Czech Republic)

Men's 100m Backstroke: I.Plotnikov (S6, Russia), L.Lamback (S7, USA), K.Lisenkov (S8, Russia), M.Cowdrey (S9, Australia), J.Zook (S10, USA), B.Yang (S11, China), A.Nevolin-Svetov (S12, Russia), C.Taiganidis (S13, Greece)

Women's 100m Backstroke: M.de Koning-Peper (S6, Netherlands), K.Porter (S7, Australia), H.Frederiksen (S8, Gt Britain), S.Dixon (S9, Canada), S.Pascoe (S10, New Zealand), C.Gotell (S13, Canada)

50m Breaststroke: T.Suzuki (SB3, Japan)

Men's 100m Breaststroke: R.Ten (SB4, Spain), P.Rangel (SB5, Mexico), A.Fomenkov (SB6, Russia), S.Kindred (SB7, Great Britain), A.Kalyna (SB8, Ukraine), K.Paul (SB9, South Africa), O.Mashchenko (SB11, Ukraine), M.Veraksa (SB12, Ukraine), O.Fedyna (SB13, Ukraine)

Women's 100m Breaststroke: B.Hlavackova (SB4, Czech Republic), K.Bruhn (SB5, Germany), E.Johnson (SB6, Great Britain), E.Popovich (SB7, USA), O.Vladykina (SB8, Russia), S.Pascoe (SB9, New Zealand), K.Pelendritou (SB12, Cyprus)

Men's 50m Butterfly: R.Perkins (S5, USA), Q.Xu (S6, China), R.Tian (S7, China)

Women's 50m Butterfly: F.Jiang (S6, China), M.Huang (S7, China)

Men's 100m Butterfly: P.Leek (S8, Australia), T.Sors (S9, Hungary), A.Brasil (S10, Brazil), E.Enhamed (S11, Spain), R.Makarau (S12, Belarus), D.Salei (S13, Belarus)

Women's 100m Butterfly: J.Long (S8, USA), N.du Toit (S9, South Africa), A.Eames (S10, USA), J.Mendak (S12, Poland), V.Grand Maison (S13, Canada)

Star athlete: Jessica Long

Born: 29/02/1992

Country: USA

Events: Women's 100m Backstroke and Butterfly – S8, women's 100m Breaststroke – SB8

Classification Category: 8

Paralympic Medals: Gold women's 100m Freestyle – S8, 400m Freestyle – S8 and 4 x 100m Freestyle Relay – 34 Points (Athens 2004); Gold women's 100m Freestyle – S8, 400m Freestyle – S8, 100m Butterfly – S8 and 200m Individual Medley – SM8, Silver women's 100m Backstroke – S8, Bronze women's 100m Breaststroke – SB8 (Beijing 2008)

Jessica Long will be just 20 when she competes at London 2012, but she has already amassed an amazing collection of medals.

She won three golds at the age of 12 at Athens 2004 before retaining her title in the 100m and 400m Freestyle – S8 at Beijing 2008. Long went on to win medals in every Swimming stroke, including golds in the 200m Individual Medley – SM8 and the 100m Butterfly – S8.

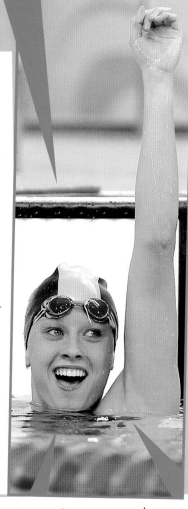

physical impairment may have more difficulty performing this stroke compared to, say, the Backstroke. Regardless of their class, swimmers require high levels of technical ability in order to keep their body in a streamlined position and move through the water quickly.

Breaststroke and Backstroke events have been a mainstay of the Paralympic Games programme ever since 25m and 50m races were held at the inaugural Rome 1960 Games. However, it was not until Toronto 1976 that Butterfly was added to the competition programme.

At the core of the Breaststroke technique is a strong kick, with the aim being to move the upper and lower body simultaneously to create a smooth action through the water. The Butterfly requires similar skills, with a 'dolphin-like' kick used to create a rhythm as swimmers pull their bodies through the water.

The Backstroke, meanwhile, is the only stroke performed on the back, where spatial awareness is particularly important in order to swim in a straight line.

The USA has a fine tradition in Swimming, with Trischa Zorn's bronze in the women's 100m Backstroke – S12 at Athens 2004 being the American's 46th medal across her amazing career. The USA led the way with the most gold medals again at Beijing 2008 with a total haul of 17, four of which were won by teenage star Jessica Long.

China won the most Swimming medals overall four years ago, with 52, and one of their stars this year is likely to be visually impaired 100m Backstroke – S11 competitor Bozun Yang, the reigning world and Paralympic Games champion.

Another star of the 100m Backstroke is Canada's Stephanie Dixon (S9), who has won the women's title at the last three Games and has 19 medals overall, including seven golds. Elsewhere, Ellie Cole (S9) will be part of a strong Australian squad that also includes multiple champions Peter Leek (S8) and Matthew Cowdrey (S9).

Classification categories

- **1-10** – Athletes with a physical impairment. The lower the number the greater the impact of the athlete's impairment on their ability to perform each stroke
- **11-13** – Athletes with a visual impairment. The lower the number the greater the level of visual impairment
- **14** – Athletes with an intellectual impairment

Each score is preceded by a letter code, depending on the event:
- **S** – Backstroke and Butterfly
- **SB** – Breaststroke

Ones to watch

1. **Sascha Kindred** (men's 100m Breaststroke – SB7, Great Britain)
2. **Bozun Yang** (men's 100m Backstroke – S11, China)
3. **Stephanie Dixon** (women's 100m Backstroke – S9, Canada)

Swimming
Freestyle, Medley and Relays

A total of 87 gold medals will be handed out at the impressive new Aquatics Centre as the best swimmers in the world aim for glory in the eagerly-anticipated Freestyle and Medley events as well as the relay races.

Multiple gold medallist Natalie du Toit.

These are some of the fastest races on the programme, and competition across all the classification categories will be particularly intense.

Freestyle is the most widely participated Swimming stroke for disabled athletes and has been included in the Games since 1960. At London 2012, a total of 63 individual Freestyle medal events will be staged, with swimmers competing in the 50m, 100m, 200m and 400m races.

The tactics used in Freestyle events differ according to the distance being swum, with competitors allowed to use any stroke. The majority favour front crawl, as it is acknowledged as being the fastest.

The 50m is the shortest Freestyle race and is a flat-out sprint based on raw power. The 100m, which is two lengths of a standard eight-lane 50-metre pool, also requires high levels of speed endurance, although equally important is the ability to turn effectively. In races over such a short distance, a good start is crucial, with quick reactions and a smooth entry into the pool potentially decisive. Swimmers, who are classified from 1-14 as part of a points-

Key facts

Venue: Aquatics Centre, London

Dates: 30 August – 8 September

Current Paralympic champions:
Men's 50m Freestyle: G.Kapellakis (S2, Greece), D.Vynohradets (S3, Ukraine), D.Smetanine (S4, France), D.Kryzhanovskyy (S5, Ukraine), Q.Xu (S6, China), D.Roberts (S7, Great Britain), X.Wang (S8, China), M.Cowdrey (S9, Australia), A.Brasil (S10, Brazil), E.Enhamed (S11, Spain), M.Veraksa (S12, Ukraine), O.Fedyna (S13, Ukraine)
Women's 50m Freestyle: P.Valle (S3, Mexico), N.Miranda (S4, Mexico), M.Teresa Perales (S5, Spain), M.de Koning-Peper (S6, Netherlands), C.Jordan (S7, USA), C.Drabsch Norland (S8, Norway), N.du Toit (S9, S.Africa), A.Polinario (S10, Canada), M.Poiani Panigati (S11, Italy), O.Savchenko (S12, Russia), K.Becherer (S13, USA)
Men's 100m Freestyle: D.Kokarev (S2, Russia), J.Du (S3, China), D.Smetanine (S4, France), D.Dias (S5, Brazil), A.Olsson (S6, Sweden), D.Roberts (S7, Great Britain), X.Wang (S8,

China), M.Cowdrey (S9, Australia), A.Brasil (S10, Brazil), E.Enhamed (S11, Spain), M.Veraksa (S12, Ukraine), C.Taiganidis (S13, Greece)
Women's 100m Freestyle: N.Miranda (S4, Mexico), M.Teresa Perales (S5, Spain), E.Simmonds (S6, Great Britain), E.Popovich (S7, USA), J.Long (S8, USA), N.du Toit (S9, S.Africa), A.Owens (S10, USA), Q.Xie (S11, China), O.Savchenko (S12, Russia), V.Grand Maison (S13, Canada)
Men's 200m Freestyle: D.Kokarev (S2, Russia), R.Oribe (S4, Spain), D.Dias (S5, Brazil)
Women's 200m Freestyle: M.Teresa Perales (S5, Spain)
Men's 400m Freestyle: A.Olsson (S6, Sweden), D.Roberts (S7, Great Britain), S.Hynd (S8, Great Britain), J.Collado (S9, Spain), A.Brasil (S10, Brazil), E.Enhamed (S11, Spain), S.Punko (S12, Belarus), C.Bouwer (S13, S.Africa)
Women's 400m Freestyle: E.Simmonds (S6, Great Britain), E.Popovich (S7, USA), J.Long (S8, USA), N.du Toit (S9, S.Africa), K.Pawlik

(S10, Poland), V.Grand Maison (S13, Canada)
Men's 150m Individual Medley: C.Leslie (SM4, New Zealand)
Women's 150m Individual Medley: K.Lauridsen (SM4, Denmark)
Men's 200m Individual Medley: D.Dias (SM5, Brazil), S.Kindred (SM6, Great Britain), R.Garcia Tolson (SM7, USA), P.Leek (SM8, Australia), M.Cowdrey (SM9, Australia), R.Pendleton (SM10, Australia), M.Veraksa (SM12, Ukraine), O.Fedyna (SM13, Ukraine)
Women's 200m Individual Medley: M.Uhl (SM6, USA), E.Popovich (SM7, USA), J.Long (SM8, USA), N.du Toit (SM9, S.Africa), S.Pascoe (SM10, New Zealand), O.Savchenko (SM12, Russia), C.Gotell (SM13, Canada)
Men's 4 x 100m Freestyle Relay – 34pts: Great Britain
Women's 4 x 100m Freestyle Relay – 34pts: N/A
Men's and Women's 4 x 100m Medley Relays – 34pts: N/A

Matthew Cowdrey was named Male Paralympian of the Year following his eight-medal haul at Beijing 2008.

The Australian won five golds and three silvers, with his standout performance coming in the final of the 50m Freestyle – S9, where he broke the world record.

Cowdrey also won three gold medals on his Paralympic Games debut at the age of just 15 at the Athens 2004 Games.

strong medal contender (S6). The first Individual Medley at the Games was staged in 1968 as a 3 x 25m race which included Breaststroke, Backstroke and Freestyle, before the Butterfly was added to the Medley in 1976. This year, there will be a 200m Individual Medley involving all of the strokes and a 150m Individual Medley with three (Butterfly being omitted).

In the relay events, the 4 x 100m Freestyle Relay – 34 Points and the 4 x 100m Medley Relay – 34 Points are both swum over four legs of 100m, with a different competitor on each.

based system, can start the race either by standing or sitting on a platform, or in the water.

There are four men's events and two for women in the 200m Freestyle, while the 400m is open to more classification categories and is the longest individual race swum at the Paralympic Games. Both events require athletes to show high levels of stamina, a good turn and plenty of tactical awareness.

Most Freestyle swimmers compete in all of the races, meaning some of the best have racked up big medal hauls. Great Britain's Mike Kenny, for example, dominated between

1976 and 1988, winning 16 golds, while France's Beatrice Hess won 19 medals, including 15 golds, from Atlanta 1996 to Athens 2004.

In more recent times, American Erin Popovich (S7) and South African Natalie du Toit (S9, featured on page 98) have dominated the Freestyle events in their respective classification categories, with the duo having won 14 and 10 gold medals. Popovich has since retired but Du Toit is hopeful of adding to her collection at London 2012, while Britain's Ellie Simmonds (featured on page 102) is also expected to be a

Daniel Dias takes the pool by storm

The Brazilian star burst onto the Paralympic Games scene at Beijing 2008 in the S5 and SM5 categories. He competed in 11 events (four of them relays) over distances of 50m, 100m and 200m. From those races he amassed a staggering four golds, four silvers and one bronze medal, making him one of the most talked-about athletes at the Games. Even more surprisingly, Dias only started training seriously at the age of 16, with all his 2008 Games medals coming only four years later, aged 20.

Table Tennis

Table Tennis was one of the original sports that appeared at the first Paralympic Games in Rome in 1960, and the fast and frenetic competition has featured as an integral part of the competition programme ever since.

Originally contested only by athletes with wheelchairs, competitions for standing players were included for the first time at Toronto 1976 and then for athletes with cerebral palsy four years later. Intellectually impaired athletes first competed at Sydney 2000 and, after being left out of the classifications in 2004 and 2008, they will return for London 2012.

The sport combines power, speed, skill and subtlety and makes for a thrilling spectacle. The aim for competitors is to hit the ball over a net – which divides the playing surface down the middle and is 15.25 centimetres high – into the opponent's half of the table in such a way that they cannot return it effectively, or at all, as in standard Tennis.

The table is 2.7 metres long and 1.52m wide and is covered with a smooth, low-friction coating, while the ball weighs only 2.7 grams. The scoring sees matches played over a best-of-five-games format, with the first player to reach 11 points, by a margin of two clear points, winning each game.

Generating spin on the ball is one of the keys to deceiving an opponent, and the rackets used have developed a great deal since the 1950s to help the game become even more dynamic and allow for some of the scintillating fast-paced rallies that are such a feature of the sport.

Table Tennis rules are tweaked for athletes who compete in wheelchairs, with each serve having to cross the back of the table before it can be returned, while athletes with an amputation or who have a hand impairment do not need to throw the ball up when serving.

Athletes with a wide range of impairments, with the exception of the blind or visually impaired, take part in Table Tennis at the

Players with a hand impairment do not need to throw the ball up when they serve.

Key facts

Venue: ExCeL, London

Dates: 30 August – 8 September

Current Paralympic champions:

Individual – Class 1: Andreas Vevera (Austria)

Individual – Class 1-2: Jing Liu (China)

Individual – Class 2: Vincent Boury (France)

Individual – Class 3: Panfeng Feng (China, men's), Qian Li (China, women's)

Individual – Class 4: Ying Zhou (China)

Individual – Class 5: Guixiang Ren (China)

Individual – Class 6: Peter Rosenmeier (Denmark)

Individual – Class 7: Jochen Wollmert (Germany)

Individual – Class 8: Gang Chen (China, men's), Thu Kamkasomphou (France, women's)

Individual – Class 9: Lina Lei (China)

Individual – Class 10: Natalia Partyka (Poland)

Individual – Class 11: N/A

Team – Class 1-2: Slovakia

Team – Class 1-3: China

Team – Class 3: France

Team – Class 4-5: China (men's), China (women's)

Team – Class 6-8: China

Team – Class 6-10: China

Team – Class 9-10: China

Star athlete: Natalia Partyka

Born: 27/06/1989

Country: Poland

Events: Women's Individual, women's Team

Classification Category: Class 10

Paralympic Medals: Gold Individual – Class 10, Silver Team – Class 6-10 (Athens 2004); Gold Individual – Class 10, Silver Team – Class 6-10 (Beijing 2008)

Natalia Partyka has been a star in Paralympic Table Tennis since making her Games debut at the age of 11 at Sydney 2000.

The Polish player will aim for a third consecutive Individual – Class 10 gold medal at London 2012 after wins in 2004 and 2008.

She will also be hoping to lead her country to gold in the Team – Class 6-10 event, having been forced to settle for silver at the last two Games.

In 2008, Partyka was one of only two athletes, along with South African swimmer Natalie du Toit, to compete at both the Olympic Games and the Paralympic Games in Beijing.

Lina Lei and Panfeng Feng are among the new generation of stars for the Chinese team, who already have Paralympic Games gold to their names and will once again be the team to beat.

The French hopes lie with a strong contingent of athletes who compete in wheelchairs, including Florian Merrien, Jean-Philippe Robin, Stephane Molliens, Vincent Boury and Maxime Thomas in the men's events, while Laos-born French player Thu Kamkasomphou is the dominant force in the women's Individual – Class 8 category.

Looking to emulate the achievements of Jane Blackburn, who won four golds and two silvers between 1972 and 1984, are the likes of Great Britain's Will Bayley and Sue Gilroy. Bayley is one of the top three players in the world at Individual – Class 7 level, while Gilroy is a two-time Commonwealth Games champion in the Individual – Class 4 category.

Classification categories

- **Class 1-5** – Athletes with a physical impairment competing in wheelchairs
- **Class 6-10** – Athletes with a physical impairment competing standing up
- **Class 11** – Athletes with an intellectual impairment

Ones to watch

1. **Yang Ge** (Individual – Class 10, China)
2. **Jing Liu** (Individual – Class 1-2, China)
3. **Maxime Thomas** (Individual – Class 4, France)

Paralympic Games and a total of 11 different classifications are used. Classes 1-5 cover athletes who use wheelchairs and classes 6-10 are for standing athletes. In both cases, the lower numbers in each class refer to those athletes with the most severe disabilities. Class 11 covers those with intellectual impairments.

At London 2012, Table Tennis will be the fourth largest sport on the programme after Athletics, Swimming and Cycling.

There will be 29 medal events and 276 athletes taking part in the Individual and Team tournaments in both the men's and women's competitions. The individual events will start in groups, where the top athletes will progress to the knockout stages, while the team events will be run in a straight knockout format.

France claimed the most Table Tennis medals at the Paralympic Games in both 1996 and 2000, but it has been China who have led the way in the sport since, dominating with a combined total of 20 gold medals in 2004 and 2008.

At Beijing 2008, China's Xiaoling Zhang competed at her sixth Games at the age of 51 and won a bronze in the women's Individual – Class 8 competition to end her amazing career with a total of nine medals, including seven golds. The likes of Yang Ge, Jing Liu,

Wheelchair Basketball

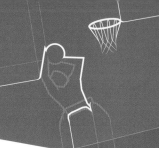

Wheelchair Basketball is widely regarded as one of the most popular disability sports in the world and the competition is expected to provide some of the most fast-paced and exhilarating action of this Games.

The sport shares the majority of its rules with its non-disabled alternative, with the same-sized courts, a 3.05-metre high hoop and no more than five players from each team allowed on the court at any one time.

Matches are played over four quarters of 10 minutes, with two points awarded for a regular shot from open play, one point for a free throw and three points for a shot from distance (6.75m or more from the basket). Players are also penalised when they keep hold of the ball while moving and they must bounce or throw the ball after every two pushes of the wheels of their chairs – the equivalent of travelling in non-disabled Basketball. On offence, players are not allowed to remain in the key area around the basket for more than three seconds without attempting a shot.

There are eight classifications for Wheelchair Basketball athletes (classes 1.0, 1.5, 2.0, 2.5, 3.0, 3.5, 4.0 and 4.5)

depending on their functional ability on the court. Athletes in class 1.0 have the least physical function and those in 4.5 have the most. The on-court classification value of the five players on a team is not allowed to exceed 14.

Wheelchair Basketball is an all-action sport and speed, vision and good hand-eye co-ordination are key attributes. Chair skills are vital and the wheelchairs are specially designed and made of titanium to ensure that they are as light as possible to manoeuvre around the court.

Such is the competitive nature of Wheelchair Basketball that collisions can often happen throughout matches and, as a result, the chairs can last for as little as six months during

periods of intense competition at the highest level.

The sport originated in the United States in the mid-1940s, when former basketball players who had been injured in World War II developed the game as a way of returning to competitive team sport.

At around the same time in Britain, Sir Ludwig Guttmann developed a similar sport called Wheelchair Netball to aid the rehabilitation for war veterans at Stoke Mandeville Hospital. Wheelchair Netball appeared for the first time at the Stoke Mandeville 1948 Games and the United States Wheelchair Basketball team, the Pan Am Jets, made their debut in the Stoke Mandeville 1955 Games. In those days, there were no backboards, although this was

Key facts

Venue: North Greenwich Arena, London; Basketball Arena, London

Dates: 30 August – 8 September

Current Paralympic champions: Australia (men's tournament), USA (women's tournament)

The United States women's team celebrate retaining their Paralympic Games title in Beijing.

Star team: Canada Men

Paralympic Medals: Gold (Sydney 2000), Gold (Athens 2004), Silver (Beijing 2008)

Eager for revenge four years on from their defeat to Australia in the final at Beijing 2008, and boosted by the return of arguably the world's best player in Patrick Anderson, Canada will be gunning for gold once more in the men's competition.

They went into the Sydney 2000 Games having never won a medal at a Paralympic Games before but then won every game on their way to the gold. Another gold followed at Athens 2004 but they failed in their attempt to become the first men's Wheelchair Basketball team to win three consecutive titles in China.

changed the following year and Wheelchair Basketball as it is known today was introduced.

The sport appeared at the first Paralympic Games at Rome 1960 with two different competitions for male athletes, both of which were won by the United States. They retained both their titles at Tokyo 1964 before the competition was reduced to just one event at Tel Aviv 1968, where an event for women was also included for the first time. Israel won both the men's and women's events on their home soil.

In the men's Wheelchair Basketball tournament, the United States have traditionally dominated, having won seven gold medals and won a medal of some sort in all but four Paralympic Games.

In recent years, their rivals, Canada, have also emerged as a force to be reckoned with. The Canadians took gold at Sydney 2000 and Athens 2004 but were denied a third successive Paralympic Games triumph at Beijing 2008 when they lost 72-60 in the final against Australia. With the influential Patrick Anderson (featured on page 96) in their ranks, Canada are sure to be a leading team once again at London 2012.

Australia won the World Championships in 2010 and will start the tournament as favourites, while the Great Britain men's Wheelchair Basketball team will be hoping for success on home soil after winning bronze at the last two Paralympic Games.

In the women's Wheelchair Basketball tournament, the United States will be aiming for a third successive gold medal. The USA defeated Germany to win the title in Beijing four years ago and did so again to win gold at the 2010 World Championships.

There will be 12 men's teams and 10 women's teams in the respective competitions. The tournaments will begin with a round-robin format involving two groups of six in the men's tournament and two groups of five in the women's. The top four teams from each group progress to the quarter-finals, at which stage the competition becomes a straight knockout.

Classification categories

- Player are assigned a point value based on their functional ability, from 1.0 with the least physical function through to 4.5 for the most. During play, the total on-court point value for each team cannot exceed 14

Ones to watch

1. **Great Britain** (women's tournament)
2. **France** (men's tournament)
3. **Australia** (men's tournament)

Wheelchair Fencing

Requiring a combination of lightning-quick reflexes and a high degree of technique, Wheelchair Fencing is likely to see some of the most frenetic action of the London 2012 Games.

The sport has evolved considerably since it was held by Paralympic Games founder Sir Ludwig Guttmann as part of competitions at Stoke Mandeville Hospital in 1953, and 12 medal events will be staged this year.

Athletes will do battle in wheelchairs that are fastened to the floor, ensuring that they are fixed in position and have freedom of movement to use their upper bodies to lunge and score points. The frames that the wheelchairs are attached to can be moved to suit right or left-handed competitors, while the length of the playing area is determined by the athlete with the shortest reach. In all events, one hand is used to hold onto the fencing weapon and the other to hold onto the chair to provide support. Fencers are required to remain seated while a bout is in progress with both feet on the footrest of their chair.

There are three types of event in Wheelchair Fencing, classified by the type of sword that is used – namely the Epée, Foil and Sabre. The Epée uses the heaviest weapon and is considered to be a true duelling sword, with fencers able to score simultaneous hits. The scoring zone is anywhere above the opponent's waist.

The Foil event also sees points scored by hitting an opponent with the tip of the weapon. However, in this class the sword is lighter and the target area is limited to an opponent's torso.

The Sabre, modelled on the traditional cavalry sword, also allows points to be scored anywhere above the waist but in this class both the tip and the edge of the blade may be used. While both genders compete in the Epée and the Foil, only the men take part in Sabre competitions. In all three types of event, fencers must wear

Classification categories

- **Category A** – Athletes with full trunk movement and good balance
- **Category B** – Athletes with impaired trunk movement and impaired balance

Ones to watch

1. **Romain Noble** (men's Epée – Category A and Sabre – Category A, France)
2. **Daoliang Hu** (men's Epée – Category B and Foil – Category B, China)
3. **Saysunee Jana** (women's Epée – Category B, Thailand)

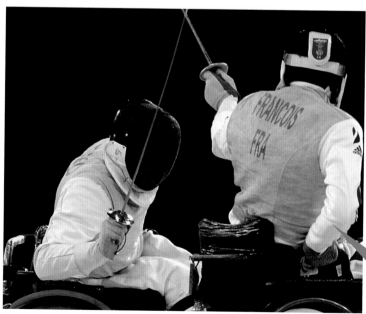

Laurent François (right) will lead France's challenge in the Sabre – Category B at London 2012.

Star athlete: Chui Yee Yu

Born: 29/03/1984

Country: Hong Kong

Events: Women's Epée, Foil and Team – Open

Classification Category: Category A

Paralympic Medals: Gold women's Foil – Category A, Epée – Category A, Team Foil and Team Epée (Athens 2004); Gold women's Foil – Category A, Silver women's Epée – Category A (Beijing 2008)

Chui Yee Yu's success in winning one gold medal and one silver medal at Beijing 2008 completed an almost perfect Games performance for Hong Kong in the women's Wheelchair Fencing competitions.

The Asian nation won three of the four gold medals available, with Yu claiming victory in the Foil – Category A and being narrowly edged out in the final of the Epée – Category A. That saw the talented fencer write another chapter in her remarkable career, having already claimed four golds at Athens 2004.

Yu will again be hoping to claim a spot on the podium at London 2012, with the team event also returning to the competition programmme.

the first team of three to score 45 hits is declared the winner. According to the rules, each team must contain at least one athlete from Category B.

China dominated the sport on home soil four years ago with a total of 13 medals, including six golds. The likes of Ruyi Ye, Daoliang Hu and Jianquan Tian followed up their Beijing success with glory at the 2010 World Championships, while Hong Kong's Yui Chong Chan and Chui Yee Yu have 10 Paralympic Games golds and two silver medals between them and will once again be expected to shine in the women's events.

France look to be the strongest European nation, with Laurent François the leading name in the Sabre – Category B, while double European champion Romain Noble is likely to be a force in the Category A event.

Key facts

Venue: ExCeL, London

Dates: 4-8 September

Current Paralympic champions:

Men's Epée – Category A: Jianquan Tian (China),

Women's Epée – Category A: Chuncui Zhang (China)

Men's Epée – Category B: Daoliang Hu (China)

Women's Epée – Category B: Yui Chong Chan (Hong Kong)

Men's Foil – Category A: Ruyi Ye (China)

Women's Foil – Category A: Chui Yee Yu (Hong Kong)

Men's Foil – Category B: Daoliang Hu (China)

Women's Foil – Category B: Yui Chong Chan (Hong Kong)

Sabre – Category A: Ruyi Ye (China)

Sabre – Category B: Laurent Francois (France)

Team – Open: N/A

protective clothing, including a mask, a jacket and gloves. A protective cover is placed on the wheelchair to prevent hits on the chair from being recorded by the electronic scoring system.

Fencers at the Paralympic Games are classified into one of two categories, depending on the level of their impairment. Category A athletes have full trunk movement and good balance and in some cases can stand or walk. Category B is for fencers who have impaired trunk movement and impaired balance but still have full use of their arms and hands.

In all Wheelchair Fencing events, competitors take part in three-minute long bouts in the preliminary rounds, with the winner being the first athlete to score five hits or the most points in the time limit allowed. In the knockout stages, fencers compete in three rounds of three minutes, with the first to 15 points declared the winner, or again the most hits in the time limit taking victory. In the event of a tie, a one-minute sudden-death bout is staged, where the first athlete to land a hit wins.

Team events will make their return to the competition programme at London 2012 after being dropped from the Beijing 2008 programme. The men and women will compete in separate Team – Open competitions, and in both events

Wheelchair Rugby

Despite its name, the high-octane and thrilling sport of Wheelchair Rugby actually has more in common with Wheelchair Basketball and Handball than it does with its non-disabled namesake that uses an oval ball.

The sport was invented by a group of Canadian quadriplegic athletes in 1977, as they were looking for an alternative to Wheelchair Basketball which would allow players with reduced arm and hand function to take part on an equal basis. What they came up with was a unique sport, where the object of the game is to carry a ball across the opposing team's goal line in a wheelchair, with two wheels having to cross the line in order for the score to count.

Wheelchair Rugby is played on a regulation-sized indoor basketball court using a white ball the same size and weight as the ones used in Sitting Volleyball. Players carry the ball in their laps and must pass or bounce it once every 10 seconds. Once a team gets possession of the ball, they have 40 seconds in which to try and score.

As in Wheelchair Basketball, a key area is designated at either end of the court, which in Wheelchair Rugby is eight metres wide by 1.75m long. Only three defenders are allowed in the key area next to the goal line at any one time,

while an attacker can only stay in this area for 10 seconds before coming back out again.

Teams are made up of four players, with up to eight substitutes allowed, and games consist of four eight-minute quarters, with three minutes of overtime played beyond that if the scores are tied.

At London 2012, the eight competing teams will be allowed up to 12 athletes, but no more than 11 of the squad can be men. Because it is classed as a mixed sport, women can take part and, at the Beijing 2008 Games, Canada, China and Great Britain each had one female member in their squad.

The competition will begin with two groups of four teams playing each other in a round-robin

format. From there, the top two teams qualify for the semi-finals, while the bottom two teams in each group compete for fifth to eighth place.

The event at the Basketball Arena will be the fourth time that Wheelchair Rugby has been included on the competition programme as a medal event. After the sport had spread throughout Canada and the United States during the 1980s, the first international event was held in 1989 between those two countries and Great Britain. A year later, the sport first appeared at the World Wheelchair Games as an exhibition event and, as it grew in popularity and participation levels increased, Wheelchair Rugby was then staged as a

Key facts

Venue: Basketball Arena, London

Dates: 5–9 September

Current Paralympic champions: USA

Collisions play a big role in the Wheelchair Rugby competition.

Paralympic Medals: Gold (Sydney 2000), Bronze (Athens 2004), Gold (Beijing 2008)

The United States will be big favourites to claim the gold medal for a third time at London 2012. Since winning the demonstration event on home soil at Atlanta 1996, they have won the Paralympics Games title at Sydney 2000 and again at Beijing 2008, with their only blip coming at Athens 2004, when they had to settle for bronze behind winners New Zealand.

The USA team has also won four out of the five World Championships since the first event in 1995.

Australia had to settle for silver behind the Americans in Beijing four years ago, where captain Bryan Kirkland and Will Groulx combined for 29 goals and 15 assists in a 53-44 victory for the USA.

demonstration event at the Atlanta Games in 1996.

Since Sydney 2000, the sport has appeared at every Games and has become one of the must-see highlights for spectators thanks to its fast-moving nature, the skill on show and also the toughness needed due to the high level of physical contact that can occur.

Contact between the wheelchairs is permitted and forms a key part of the game, with many collisions taking place as players attempt to stop their opponents and take control of the ball. Hitting an opponent's chair from behind is not permitted, however, while physical contact between players is also not allowed. Due to the nature of the sport, the wheelchairs are specially modified so that they are strong enough to protect players, while

also being lightweight and easy to manoeuvre. To be eligible to play Wheelchair Rugby, athletes must have an impairment that affects the arms and the legs, known as quadriplegia or tetraplegia, and they must also be able to push a manual wheelchair with their arms.

Players are given a classification depending on their upper-body function, which ranges from 0.5 to 3.5, with the higher of the seven scores corresponding to those athletes with the most physical function. During a game, the total value of all the players on court for a team cannot exceed eight points, ensuring teams field a mix of athletes with varying levels of impairment.

The United States are the reigning Paralympic Games champions, but they will be pushed all the way by the likes

of Australia and Japan, who did well at the 2010 World Championships by finishing in second and third place respectively behind the USA.

Classification categories

- Every player is assigned a point value based on their functional ability, from 0.5 with the least physical function through to 3.5 for the most physical function. During play, the total on-court point value for each team of five players cannot exceed 8

Ones to watch

1. Japan
2. Great Britain
3. Australia

Wheelchair Tennis

The sport of Wheelchair Tennis continues to grow at a rapid rate, and that is little wonder with matches often action-packed and full of high drama that has the crowd on the edge of their seats.

This is an exciting sport in which athletes require high levels of skill, fitness and strategy to enjoy success. The only difference from non-disabled tennis is that the ball is allowed to bounce twice after it has come across the net, with the first bounce having to be within the set court boundaries. Other than this, the two sports follow the same rules, with competitors aiming to hit the ball into their opponent's half of the court so that they are unable to return it.

Wheelchair Tennis can be played on a regular court without any special modifications needed to either the size, or the rackets and balls. Games are played on a best-of-three sets basis, with a tie-break used to decide the winner of a set if it is level at 6-6. The

sport will be making its sixth appearance as a medal event at London 2012. It was first introduced in the USA in 1976, with founders Brad Parks and Jeff Minnenbraker playing and promoting it across the United States. Parks, who used the sport in his rehabilitation after he was left paralysed following a skiing accident, was the first president of the International Wheelchair Tennis Federation, set up in 1988, the same year the sport was included as a demonstration event in Seoul.

At Barcelona 1992, the sport made its debut as a medal event at the Paralympic Games and firmly caught the public's imagination, as 32 men from 15

nations and 16 women players from nine different countries competed. The International Tennis Federation (ITF) is now the main governing body for the sport, which is played by athletes in more than 100 countries across the world, with the top players competing at all the major Grand Slams, as well as the Paralympic Games.

To compete, athletes must have a permanent, substantial or total loss of function in one or both of their legs. The Quad classification, meanwhile, requires players to have an impairment in three or more limbs, with quadriplegic athletes featuring at the Paralympic Games for the first time at

Key facts

Venue: Eton Manor, London
Dates: 1–8 September
Current Paralympic champions:
Singles: Shingo Kunieda
    (Japan, men's), Esther Vergeer
    (Netherlands, women's)
Doubles: Stephane Houdet and
    Michael Jeremiasz (France,
    men's), Korie Homan and Sharon
    Walraven (Netherlands, women's)
Singles – Quad: Peter Norfolk (GB)
Doubles – Quad: Nick Taylor and
    David Wagner (USA)

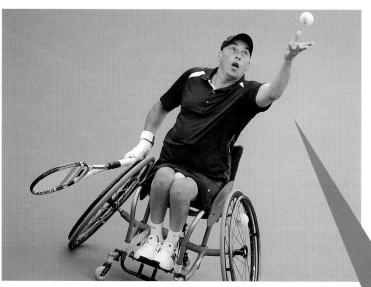

Great Britain's Peter Norfolk has won the Singles – Quad at each of the last two Games.

Star athlete: Shingo Kunieda

Born: 21/2/1984

Country: Japan

Events: Men's Singles and Doubles

Classification Category: N/A

Paralympic Medals: Gold men's Doubles (Athens 2004); Gold men's Singles, Bronze men's Doubles (Beijing 2008)

Shingo Kunieda started his career aged 11 and became Japan's first professional player in 1989. From there, he quickly established himself as one of the leading lights in the men's game, winning Doubles gold at Athens 2004 to announce his arrival on the Paralympic Games stage.

It is in Singles competition that he has really excelled, and he followed up four years later with gold in that category at Beijing 2008, as well as claiming the bronze medal in the men's Doubles competition.

He went one better at the 2010 Asian Para Games, claiming gold in both the Singles and Doubles competitions, and he will head into London 2012 as a firm favourite for more success.

won a bronze in the Doubles at Beijing 2008 to go with his gold in the same event in 2004. Dutchman Maikel Scheffers won a bronze in the Singles in 2008 and is ranked as one of the best Doubles players on the Wheelchair Tennis Tour. Scheffers and Frenchman Stephane Houdet will be two of the leading contenders trying to prevent Kunieda from increasing his Paralympic Games medal haul to four.

At Athens 2004, Peter Norfolk won Great Britain's first-ever gold medal in Wheelchair Tennis with his victory in the Singles – Quad. Norfolk successfully defended his title in 2008 and also won a bronze in the Doubles – Quad event, to go with the silver he had won four years earlier. The Great Britain athlete, who will be 41 when he competes in London, is one of the outstanding Quad players in the world, along with top American David Wagner.

Classification categories

- To compete in Wheelchair Tennis, athletes need to have a major or total loss of function in one or both legs. Players in the Quad category have an impairment that affects three or more limbs

Ones to watch

1. **Esther Vergeer** (women's Singles and Doubles, Netherlands)
2. **Peter Norfolk** (men's Singles – Quad and Doubles – Quad, Great Britain)
3. **Maikel Scheffers** (men's Singles and Doubles, Netherlands)

Athens 2004. At London 2012, there will be six medal events staged at Eton Manor, at the north end of the Olympic Park. Men and women play in both Singles and Doubles competitions, while the Singles – Quad and Doubles – Quad are mixed-gender events, where women and men battle against each other or in the same pairing. Competitions are staged in a knockout format, with players seeded based on their past performances.

Good technique is a must and one player who has demonstrated this better than anyone is Esther Vergeer of the Netherlands (featured on page 105). Vergeer has been a dominant force in the women's game and will be a hot favourite to win gold medals in both the Singles and Doubles competitions, as she bids to add to her medal haul of five gold and one silver since Sydney 2000. The Dutch have enjoyed great success at the Games, having won a total of 22 medals, and Chantal Vandierendonck and Maaike Smit are two other multiple medal winners to come from the Netherlands.

Japan's Shingo Kunieda is the best men's player in the world. He is the defending Paralympic Games champion and also

Esther Vergeer wins a third straight Wheelchair Tennis Singles title

When Esther Vergeer made her Paralympic Games debut at Sydney 2000, nobody could have predicted that she was starting out on a journey that would lead to her becoming the dominant force in women's Wheelchair Tennis for the next decade and beyond. The Dutch athlete (featured on page 105), just 19 at the time, did not lose a set as she stormed to the gold medal in both the Singles and the Doubles events, winning the latter with her partner Maaike Smit. That was the start of a spectacular rise that included further individual triumphs at Athens 2004 and Beijing 2008, as well as another Doubles success in the Greek capital as part of a lengthy unbeaten streak.

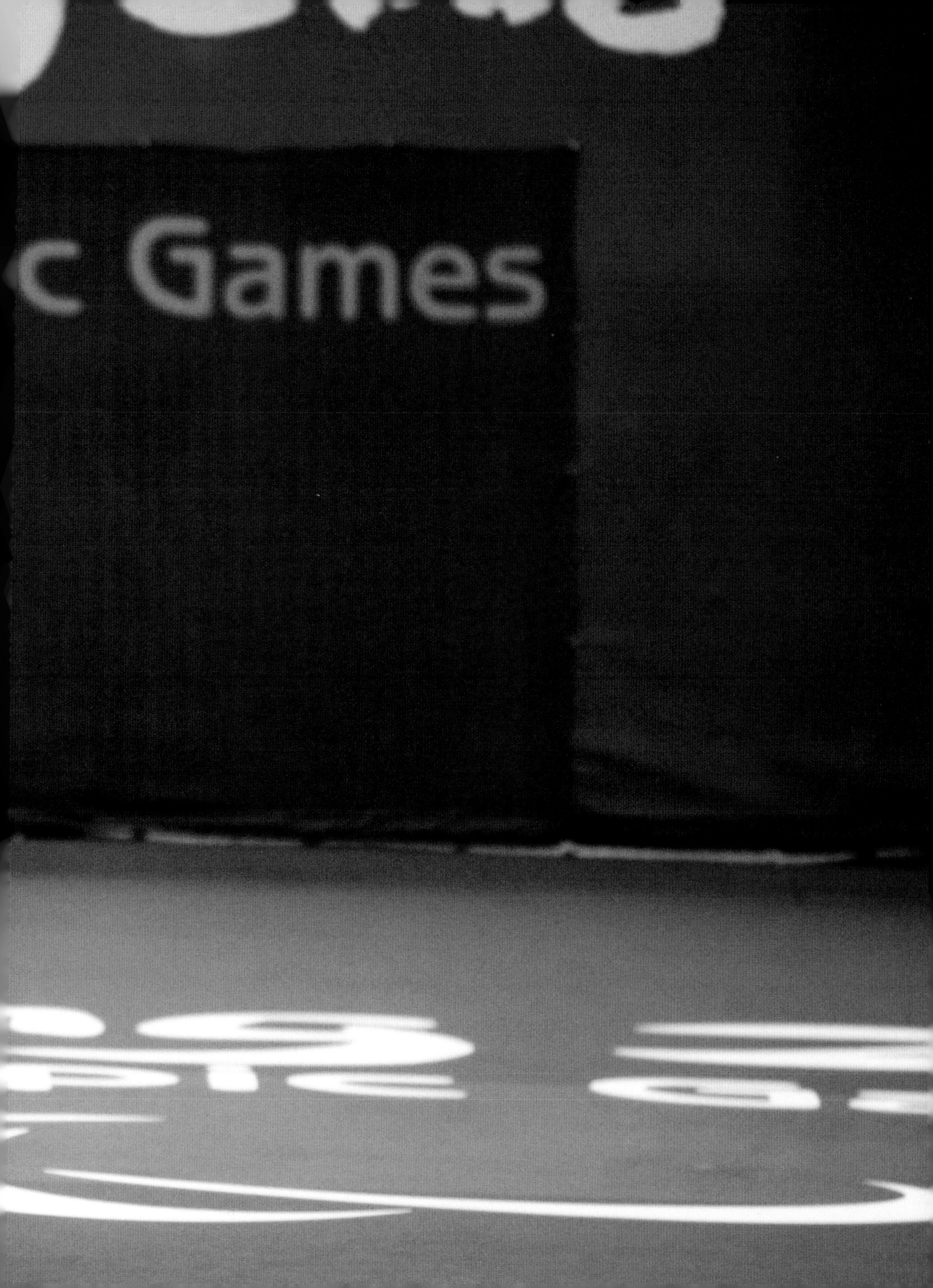
c Games

Superstars for 2012

The Paralympic Games have borne witness to some remarkable sporting feats, and more history is likely to be made at London 2012. This Games will feature a real mix of talent, from emerging athletes who will be making their debut on this stage to several multiple gold medal winners who are among the most decorated Paralympians of all time. In this chapter, we throw the spotlight on those competitors who will be bidding to join the long list of Paralympic Games greats.

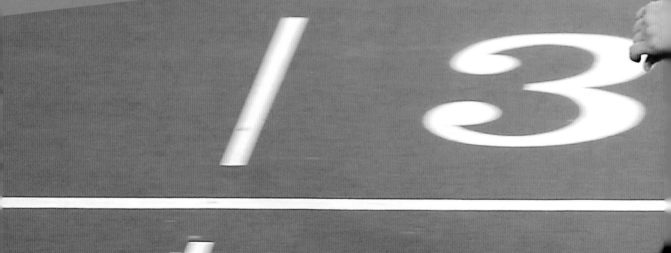

South African runner Oscar Pistorius wins gold at Beijing 2008.

Patrick Anderson
Wheelchair Basketball (Canada)

Patrick Anderson is one of the greatest players ever to grace a Wheelchair Basketball court and he will have a major role to play in Canada's bid to regain their Paralympic Games title this year.

Anderson has won virtually every major honour in the sport and he will head to London determined to erase the disappointment of having been forced to settle for silver four years ago.

When he lost both his legs above the knee in an accident, Anderson discovered Wheelchair Basketball and worked his way into the Canada junior team. His progress continued at a staggering rate and in 1997 he was named the Most Valuable Player (MVP) as Canada won the World Junior Championships and by 1998 he had become a member of Canada's senior team.

His impact at senior level was immediate, and he was soon named in the All-Star team for the 1998 World Championships after helping Canada to win a bronze medal. He arrived at Sydney 2000 as one of Canada's most respected players.

It proved to be a Paralympic Games debut to remember, as Anderson played an integral role in helping Canada to win gold with victory over the Netherlands in the final. Another MVP award and gold medal followed at the 2001 World Junior Championships, and his talents soon attracted the attention of clubs around the world.

Anderson played for the Brisbane Spinning Bullets in Australia and earned recognition for his displays by being named

Canada forward Patrick Anderson.

MVP of the Australian National Wheelchair Basketball League in 2003. And when Canada took on Australia in the final of the Athens 2004 Games, he used all his experience to score 13 points and grab 13 rebounds, as well as seven assists, as the North Americans won 70-53 to claim a second successive gold medal.

A move to the domestic league in Germany followed, where Anderson became a key player for the RSV Lahn-Dill side that won three successive European Champions Cup titles from 2004 to 2006. He also added a World Championships title in 2006 and another MVP award.

Canada were expected to win a third successive gold medal at Beijing 2008, but they were beaten by Australia 72-60 in the final, despite Anderson top-scoring with 22 points. Following that, he took a break from the sport to pursue other interests – in particular a career in music – and in his absence Canada struggled and only finished seventh at the 2010 World Championships.

With London 2012 fast approaching, a rejuvenated Anderson returned for Team Canada in 2011 and he has since helped them to win gold at the BT Paralympic World Cup in Manchester. The athletic forward will be the man to watch when Canada go in search of a third Paralympic Games gold medal.

Statistics

Born: 22/08/1979

Classification: 4.5

Paralympic Medals:
Sydney 2000: Gold
Athens 2004: Gold
Beijing 2008: Silver

Ryley Batt
Wheelchair Rugby (Australia)

Wheelchair Rugby is not for the faint-hearted and in Ryley Batt, Australia have one of the toughest competitors around and a man who is determined to finally end his wait for a Paralympic Games gold medal.

Batt was born without legs but astonishingly, the Australian did not use a wheelchair until the age of 12, using a skateboard to get around instead. A Wheelchair Rugby demonstration at his school convinced him to use a wheelchair and he has never looked back.

In 2002, Batt got his first taste of competitive action with the New South Wales Wheelchair Rugby squad and, just a year later, at the age of 13, he was called up to represent Australia in the Oceania Championships in Japan. Batt helped Australia win gold and in his first season for New South Wales he was named the Australian National Wheelchair Rugby League's Most Valuable Player (MVP).

During his early career, Batt was classified as a 2.5 – a mid-pointer in the Australian team. However, ahead of Athens 2004 he was reclassified as a 3.5. Given that the classification system in Wheelchair Rugby means that the total value of all the players on the court at any one time cannot exceed eight points, this meant he was required to take on more responsibility to justify his place in the side.

Another gold and another MVP award followed in 2007 as Australia won the Oceania Championship in Sydney. By now, Batt had established a reputation as one of the best Wheelchair Rugby players in the world and he

Ryley Batt (left) has become one of the world's leading Wheelchair Rugby players.

inspired New South Wales to the National Championship again in 2007 and 2008.

At Beijing 2008, the youngster played his part in guiding Australia to the gold medal match, where they were beaten 53-44 by the USA. Batt then took on a new challenge by going to America to play for the San Diego Sharps, who then went on to win their first US National title.

Another title followed in 2010 for the Sharps with Batt once again the inspiration, claiming another MVP award. He also continued to play for New South Wales back home and helped them to a fourth title in 2010.

Another international duel with the USA came in the final of the

2010 World Wheelchair Rugby Championships in Vancouver, although once again Australia were defeated, 57-45.

Success has continued for the talented Australian and in 2011 he was part of the New South Wales team that won a sixth consecutive National Championship. This year, he will head to London bidding for the Paralympic Games gold medal that has so far eluded him.

Statistics

Born: 22/05/1989

Classification: 3.5

Paralympic Medals:
Beijing 2008: Silver

Natalie du Toit

Swimming (South Africa)

Natalie du Toit has become an iconic and inspirational figure in South African sport over the past decade and at the London 2012 Games she will be aiming to write the final chapter of her glittering career.

Natalie du Toit has excelled across non-disabled and disabled competition.

Du Toit began swimming internationally when she was only 14 and competed in the 1998 Commonwealth Games in Kuala Lumpur. She missed out on qualification for the Olympic Games in 2000 before, in February 2001, at the age of 17, she was hit by a car while riding her scooter after a training session, forcing doctors to amputate her left leg at the knee.

Her thoughts immediately turned to when she could return to swimming and just three months later, before she had even learned to walk again, Du Toit was back in the pool. Her determination, dedication and talent saw her compete in the 2002 Commonwealth Games in Manchester just a year after her accident. She achieved sporting history when she qualified for the final of the 800m Freestyle, becoming the first athlete with an impairment to qualify for the final of a non-disabled event.

Du Toit also announced herself as a force to be reckoned with by breaking the world records on her way to winning both the multi-disability 50m Freestyle and 100m Freestyle events. She continued her success by beating non-disabled athletes to win the 800m Freestyle at the 2003 All-Africa Games. Du Toit missed out on qualification for the Athens 2004 Olympic Games but became one of the stars of the Paralympic Games in Greece by winning five golds and one silver.

She continued to dominate in the pool in 2006, retaining both her Commonwealth Games titles and powering her way to six gold medals at the IPC World Swimming Championships in front of a home crowd in Durban.

By finishing fourth in the 10km Open Water race at the Open Water World Championships in Spain in May 2008, Du Toit qualified for the Beijing 2008 Olympic Games, and in China she became the first amputee to compete in both the Olympic and Paralympic Games, finishing 16th in the women's Olympic Swimming 10km Marathon race.

Undoubtedly the world's top S9 category swimmer, Du Toit also retained her five Paralympic Games titles that year with a series of impressive displays, particularly in the 100m Butterfly – S9, where she broke the world record. Six golds followed at the 2010 World Championships and later that year she was awarded the Laureus World Sports Award for Sportsperson of the Year with a Disability.

Du Toit has stated that the London 2012 Games will be her last major event.

Statistics

Born: 29/01/1984

Classification: 9

Paralympic Medals:
Athens 2004: Gold women's 50m Freestyle – S9, 100m Freestyle – S9, 400m Freestyle – S9, 100m Butterfly – S9 and 200m Individual Medley – SM9, Silver women's 100m Backstroke – S9
Beijing 2008: Gold women's 50m Freestyle – S9, 100m Freestyle – S9, 400m Freestyle – S9, 100m Butterfly – S9 and 200m Individual Medley – SM9

Jonas Jacobsson
Shooting (Sweden)

Most athletes can only dream of winning gold at the Paralympic Games but for Jonas Jacobsson that dream has become a reality on no fewer than 16 occasions – and the Swede is not finished yet.

Undoubtedly the greatest disabled shooter of all time, London 2012 will be his ninth Games, during which time he has become one of the most decorated athletes of all time. Jacobsson's haul of 16 gold, one silver and eight bronze medals has marked him out as one of the finest Paralympians ever, and he will become the all-time leading male medal winner if he makes it onto the podium more than once in London.

Jacobsson began his Paralympic Games career at Arnhem 1980 where, at the age of 15, he won the first of his gold medals in the mixed Air Rifle Standing – 2-5 and also a bronze in the mixed Air Rifle 3 Positions — 2-5.

Jonas Jacobsson has shot to 16 golds.

Four years later, he won another gold in the men's Air Rifle Standing Team competition at the Stoke Mandeville and New York 1984 Games, while also adding a silver and a bronze from his other events.

At Seoul 1988, Jacobsson showed his amazing sporting versatility when he was part of the Sweden squad that reached the last eight of the Wheelchair Basketball competition.

Jacobsson continued his gold rush in the Shooting by helping Sweden win the Air Rifle Prone Team – 2-6 event.

He continued his successful run at Barcelona 1992 in both the mixed Olympic Match – SH2 and the Air Rifle Standing – SH2 events, before another double followed at Atlanta 1996.

He celebrated 20 years of Paralympic Games competition at Sydney 2000 by claiming two more golds and two bronzes.

Despite competing at the highest level for so long, Jacobsson showed at Athens 2004 that he had not lost his desire to win and went on to enjoy his most successful Games so far, winning four golds and breaking three world records.

It came as no surprise when he took his gold tally to 16 at Beijing 2008 by winning the Air Rifle Standing – SH1, Free Rifle 3x40 – SH1 and Free Rifle Prone – SH1 events.

Statistics

Born: 22/06/1965

Classification: SH1

Paralympic Medals:
Arnhem 1980: Gold mixed Air Rifle Standing – 2-5, Bronze mixed Air Rifle 3 Positions – 2-5
Stoke Mandeville/New York 1984: Gold men's Air Rifle Standing Team – 1A-6, Silver men's Air Rifle Standing – 2-6, Bronze men's Air Rifle 3 Positions 2-6
Seoul 1988: Gold mixed Air Rifle Prone Team – 2-6, Bronze mixed Air Rifle Standing Team – 2-6 and mixed Air Rifle 3 Positions Team – 2-6
Barcelona 1992: Gold men's Air Rifle Standing – SH2 and mixed Olympic Match – SH2, Bronze mixed Air Rifle 3x40 – SH2
Atlanta 1996: Gold mixed English Match – SH1 and men's Air Rifle 3x40 – SH1, Bronze mixed Air Rifle Prone – SH1
Sydney 2000: Gold men's Free Rifle 3x40 – SH1 and mixed Free Rifle Prone – SH1, Bronze mixed Air Rifle Prone – SH1 and men's Air Rifle Standing – SH1
Athens 2004: Gold men's Air Rifle Standing – SH1, men's Free Rifle 3x40 – SH1, mixed Air Rifle Prone – SH1 and mixed Free Rifle Prone – SH1
Beijing 2008: Gold men's Air Rifle Standing – SH1, men's Free Rifle 3x40 – SH1 and mixed Free Rifle Prone – SH1

Lee Pearson
Equestrian (Great Britain)

Few athletes are able to claim a perfect Paralympic Games record but Lee Pearson can, and at London 2012 he will be aiming for more of the same.

With nine gold medals from three Games, the 38-year-old will be one of the hot favourites to claim victory for hosts Great Britain in the Equestrian events.

Pearson began riding ponies as a child and, after watching Great Britain begin their domination of the Team – Open event by winning gold at Atlanta 1996, he embarked on his quest to compete in the sport at the highest level. Four years later, he was named in the Great Britain squad for Sydney 2000, where he won Dressage gold medals in the Championships Test: Individual and the Freestyle Test: Individual events, as well as helping Team GB to retain their Team – Open title.

One of the horses Pearson rode as part of his preparation for Sydney 2000 was Blue Circle Boy, and together they went on to win three golds at the Para-Equestrian Dressage European Championships in 2002. The pair continued to enjoy a successful partnership and a year later, Pearson became the first disabled rider to win a national title at the British Dressage Championships.

By the time the Athens 2004 Games came around, Pearson had established himself as one of the top disabled riders in the world, and once again he produced some stunning displays aboard Blue Circle Boy to win three golds in the Greek capital. Back home, his achievements were recognised by the Queen, who awarded him the Order of the British Empire (OBE) in 2005, while he was also nominated for the Laureus World Sports Award for Sportsperson of the Year with a Disability.

At Beijing 2008, Pearson was aboard a different horse, Gentleman, but his routines continued to impress the judges, who rewarded him with another two gold medals in the Championships Test: Individual and the Freestyle Test: Individual competitions. He was also an integral part of the British quartet that maintained their 100 per cent record in the team event.

With nine gold medals in his trophy cabinet, Pearson was invited to Buckingham Palace again in 2009, where he was

Lee Pearson astride Gentleman in 2008.

appointed a Commander of the Order of the British Empire (CBE).

Para-Dressage was included as part of the FEI World Equestrian Games in Kentucky in 2010 and Pearson was once again at his very best on Gentleman, winning two individual gold medals and the customary team gold.

He suffered a major blow in June 2011 when he broke his back, forcing him to miss the European Championships, but he was soon back in the saddle and will head to London 2012 as a major contender for more gold.

Statistics

Born: 04/02/1974

Classification: Ib

Paralympic Medals:
Sydney 2000: Gold Championships Test: Individual – Grade I, Freestyle Test: Individual – Grade I and Team – Open
Athens 2004: Gold Championships Test: Individual – Grade I, Freestyle Test: Individual – Grade I and Team – Open
Beijing 2008: Gold Championships Test: Individual – Grade Ib, Freestyle Test: Individual – Grade Ib and Team – Open

Oscar Pistorius
Athletics (South Africa)

As the most recognisable and high-profile Paralympic Games athlete in the world, South African sprinter Oscar Pistorius will attract plenty of attention and headlines when he takes to the track this year.

The 'Blade Runner', as he is known due to the distinctive carbon-fibre prosthetic blades he uses to compete, has become one of the great success stories in the history of the Paralympic Games.

Rehabilitation from a sports injury first led him to competitive running in January 2004.

Just eight months later, in his first Paralympic Games at Athens 2004, Pistorius won bronze in the 100m – T44 final, although it was in the 200m – T44 event where he really shone. Despite falling in the preliminary round, the South African managed to get up and still qualify for the final, where he broke the world record with a time of 21.97. He built on that success at the 2006 IPC World Athletics Championships, winning gold in the 100m, 200m and 400m – T44 events and breaking his own 200m world record in the semi-final and also the 400m world record.

Pistorius also competed against non-disabled athletes but with the Beijing 2008 Olympic Games

Star South African sprinter Oscar Pistorius.

on the horizon, the International Association of Athletics Federations (IAAF) ruled that his prostheses gave him an advantage over other athletes and he was ruled ineligible for non-disabled competition. Pistorius subsequently had that ruling overturned by the Court of Arbitration for Sport (CAS) but failed to qualify for Beijing 2008.

However, at the Paralympic Games the same year he cemented his reputation as the world's top T44 athlete, retaining his gold medal in the 200m and winning both the 100m and 400m, smashing his 400m world record in the process. That made him the first Paralympian to win gold in all three sprint events. His form continued at the 2011 IPC World Athletics Championships,

where he retained his world titles in the 200m and 400m, although he did suffer his first defeat in seven years in the 100m when American Jerome Singleton forced him into second place.

Pistorius recovered from that defeat in style, and a personal best of 45.07 in the 400m at a meeting in Lignano gave him the 'A' standard qualification time for the 2011 non-disabled World Championships and the London 2012 Olympic Games.

Pistorius was eliminated in the 400m semi-finals at the World Championships but helped South Africa to the 4 x 400m Relay final, in which they claimed silver. He was not selected for the final but his heat run entitled him to become the first Paralympian to win a non-disabled world track medal.

Statistics

Born: 22/11/1986

Classification: T44

Paralympic Medals:
Athens 2004: Gold men's 200m – T44, Bronze men's 100m – T44
Beijing 2008: Gold men's 100m – T44, 200m – T44 and 400m – T44

Ellie Simmonds
Swimming (Great Britain)

Ellie Simmonds emerged as the golden girl of British Paralympic Swimming in Beijing four years ago and the teenage sensation will be a strong favourite to land more success in the pool in front of her home crowd.

Ellie Simmonds hit the headlines after her performances in Beijing.

Simmonds has enjoyed a meteoric rise to become one of the world's top S6 competitors. The 17-year-old began swimming at the age of five and was inspired by seeing fellow British swimmer Nyree Lewis win two gold medals at Athens 2004. She quickly began to achieve National Development Squad qualification times and was only 12 when she was selected for the Great Britain team for the 2006 IPC World Championships.

Such was Simmonds' talent that her family decided to move from the West Midlands to Swansea in Wales to give her more access to world-class facilities and coaching. The move paid dividends, and at 13 she was the youngest member of the Great Britain squad for Beijing 2008.

As the second youngest British Paralympian ever, Beijing 2008 was supposed to be a learning curve for Simmonds, but she exceeded all expectations. She

took gold in both the 100m Freestyle – S6 and the 400m Freestyle – S6 events and earned a place in the history books as Great Britain's youngest-ever individual medallist at the Paralympic Games. Her tears of joy charmed audiences around the world and she became one of the stars of the event.

Glory in the pool put Simmonds firmly in the spotlight, and later that year she was named the BBC Young Sports Personality of the Year. An even greater honour followed in February 2009 when, aged 14, she became the youngest person to be appointed a Member of the Order of the British Empire (MBE).

With two gold medals and a meeting with the Queen, Simmonds could have been forgiven for getting carried away, but under the watchful eye of coach Billy Pye she has gone from strength to strength. She broke the world record in the

100m Freestyle – S6 on her way to gold at the 2009 Paralympic World Cup in Manchester and dominated her category at the 2010 IPC World Championships in Eindhoven. Not only did Simmonds sweep the board with four golds, but she also broke the world record in the 100m Freestyle – S6, 400m Freestyle – S6 and 200m Individual Medley – SM6. Her victory in the 50m Freestyle – S6 in Eindhoven was all the sweeter for beating home favourite and her biggest rival in the category, Mirjam de Koning-Peper.

Having laid down that marker, Simmonds went head-to-head with De Koning-Peper again in the 2011 IPC European Swimming Championships, and the youngster showed her class by breaking her own world records to take gold in the 400m Freestyle – S6 and 200m Individual Medley – SM6. De Koning-Peper gained revenge by beating her to gold in the 100m Freestyle – S6 on the last day of competition but the two will meet again in London ready for another fierce battle.

Statistics

Born: 11/11/1994

Classification: 6

Paralympic Medals:
Beijing 2008: Gold women's 100m Freestyle – S6 and 400m Freestyle – S6

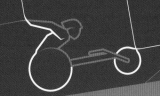

Jason Smyth
Athletics (Ireland)

With the tag of 'The world's fastest Paralympian' already to his name, Irish sprint king Jason Smyth will once again be looking to storm his way to more gold medal success on the track at London 2012.

Having claimed a memorable double in the 100m – T13 and 200m – T13 in Beijing four years ago, breaking both world records on his way to victory, Smyth is once again expected to be one of the stars of the Games.

The sprinter was only eight when he suffered a partial loss of sight but his athletic potential was clear. In 2004, he was selected to compete for Northern Ireland and participated in the Junior Commonwealth Games.

Under coach Stephen Maguire, Smyth then blew the opposition away at the 2005 IPC European Championships, breaking two world records to win both the 100m and 200m – T13 events.

Smyth then turned his attention to the IPC World Athletics Championships a year later, where he was once again unbeatable, as he broke his own world records with another phenomenal sprint double.

A matter of weeks after Usain Bolt's stunning performance at the Beijing 2008 Olympic Games, Smyth drew comparisons with the Jamaican's historic achievements and made his own mark as the Paralympic Games sprint king. He broke his own 100m and 200m world records in the heats, before doing the same in the finals to claim gold in spectacular fashion.

Not one to rest on his laurels, he subsequently moved to Florida to train with Lance Brauman and

Double Beijing gold medallist Jason Smyth.

his squad of superstar sprinters, including American Olympic Games ace Tyson Gay. It paid dividends as in 2010 Smyth made history by becoming the first Paralympian to compete at a non-disabled European Championships, finishing fourth in the semi-final, making him the 14th fastest sprinter in Europe.

Smyth had hoped to compete in

the 2010 Commonwealth Games, but a back injury curtailed his progress and also kept him out of the 2011 IPC World Athletics Championships. However, once fit again, he broke his own 100m world record in May 2011 with a time of 10.22 at a meeting in Florida. That gave Smyth the 'B' standard qualification mark for the Olympic Games, and he went to the non-disabled World Championships in August 2011, where he narrowly missed out on qualifying for the semi-final.

Smyth will be looking to go even faster in the Olympic Stadium at London 2012, where he has the chance to write his name into Paralympic Games history.

Statistics

Born: 04/07/1987

Classification: T13

Paralympic Medals:
Beijing 2008: Gold men's 100m – T13 and 200m – T13

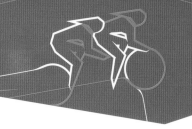

Sarah Storey
Cycling (Great Britain)

At Beijing 2008, Sarah Storey joined a select group of athletes who have won gold in two different sports at the Paralympic Games, and she is being tipped to add to her medal tally in London.

Storey's achievements have been spectacular. The 34-year-old made her name as a world-class swimmer before becoming a Cycling star within a few years of taking up the sport.

Storey excelled in the pool as a teenager and was fast-tracked into the Great Britain squad for the Barcelona 1992 Games. Although still only 14, Storey was one of the stars of the British team and won two golds in the 100m Backstroke – S10 and 200m Individual Medley – SM10, as well as three silvers and a bronze. Four years later, in Atlanta, she retained both titles and added gold in the 100m Breaststroke – SB10, before she won two silvers at Sydney 2000 and another two silvers and a bronze at Athens 2004.

However, a persistent ear infection halted her pool career

Versatile sportswoman Sarah Storey.

in 2005. Storey initially began cycling as a means of keeping fit but by the end of her first year in the sport she had broken the world record to win gold in the 3000m Individual Pursuit at the European Championships, as well as claiming another two golds in the Road Race and 500m Time Trial.

She switched full-time to Cycling and broke the world record in the 3000m Individual Pursuit once again at the 2006 World Championships. Then, at the Beijing 2008 Paralympic Games, she made history by taking gold in the 3000m Individual Pursuit in another world record time, and also won gold in the Time Trial on the road.

Storey has also competed regularly against non-disabled athletes. Just a few days after Beijing, she went on to beat a non-disabled field to win the 3000m Individual Pursuit title at the British Track Nationals and retained her crown a year later. Storey also became the first disabled cyclist to appear for England in non-disabled competition at the 2010 Commonwealth Games, where she finished sixth in the Individual Pursuit event.

Last year, she retained all her world titles on both road and track and was part of the women's team that narrowly missed out on a world record in the non-disabled Team Pursuit event at a World Cup meeting in Manchester.

Statistics

Born: 26/10/1977

Classification: C5

Paralympic Swimming Medals:
Barcelona 1992: Gold women's 100m Backstroke – S10 and 200m Individual Medley – SM10, Silver women's 400m Freestyle – S10, 4 × 100m Freestyle Relay – S7-10 and 4 × 100m Medley Relay – S7-10, Bronze women's 100m Freestyle – S10
Atlanta 1996: Gold women's 100m Backstroke – S10, 100m Breaststroke – SB10 and 200m

Individual Medley – SM10, Silver women's 400m Freestyle – S10, Bronze women's 100m Freestyle – S10
Sydney 2000: Silver women's 100m Backstroke – S10 and 4 x 100m Medley Relay – 34pts
Athens 2004: Silver women's 100m Breaststroke – SB9 and 200m Individual Medley – SM10, Bronze women's 100m Freestyle – S10
Paralympic Cycling Medals:
Beijing 2008: Gold Time Trial LC1-2/CP4 and Individual Pursuit LC1-2/CP4

Esther Vergeer
Wheelchair Tennis (Netherlands)

Many athletes can lay claim to being champions in their sport and many have even been described as being the world's best, but very few have dominated their field in the way that Esther Vergeer has in Wheelchair Tennis.

The Dutch star has put together one of the longest winning streaks in professional sport. In January 2003, Vergeer began a run of more than 420 matches without defeat in Singles competition.

Vergeer started out playing Wheelchair Basketball, winning the European Championships in 1997 as a member of the Dutch national side.

In those early days, she divided her time between Wheelchair Basketball and Wheelchair Tennis, before opting to pursue the latter full-time in 1998. The move immediately paid dividends, and she announced her arrival on the world stage with victory in both the Doubles and Singles competitions at the US Open that year. In October 1998, she moved to the top of the world rankings in the Doubles and by April the following year was also world number one in Singles.

It was not long before Vergeer graced the Paralympic Games

Esther Vergeer has more than 650 career wins and 150 individual titles to her name.

at Sydney 2000, and she did so with great success. She did not drop a set on her way to victory in both the Singles and the Doubles competitions, the latter alongside partner Maaike Smit.

By the time she faced Australia's Daniela Del Toro in the quarter-finals of the Sydney International in January 2003, it had been nearly two years since she had been beaten in a Singles match, but she surprisingly lost in straight sets. That was to be the last time that such an occurrence would happen for a very long time, though, as she soon embarked on the start of her unbeaten run.

At Athens 2004, Vergeer stormed to two golds once again, and to make the achievement even more special, she did so without losing a set. That was part of 250 consecutive sets won from August

2004 to October 2006, of which only one went to a tie-break.

Against that background, it was little surprise that by the time that she arrived at Beijing 2008, it was seen as almost a given that she would sweep past every opponent. There was a brief scare in the final of the Singles, when compatriot Korie Homan levelled the match at one set all, but Vergeer went on to win the deciding set 7-6 to secure yet another gold medal.

In the Doubles, there was rare disappointment when she suffered defeat in the final alongside Jiiske Griffioen, yet Vergeer soon brushed that off, and since the last Games she has continued to excel with the help of new coach Sven Groeneveld, to the point that she now has more than 650 career wins and 150 individual titles.

Statistics

Born: 18/07/1981

Classification: N/A

Paralympic Medals:
Sydney 2000: Gold women's
  Singles and Doubles
Athens 2004: Gold women's
  Singles and Doubles
Beijing 2008: Gold women's
  Singles, Silver women's Doubles

Paralympic Games records

Ever since the first official event took place in Rome in 1960, the Paralympic Games have provided a stage for disabled athletes around the world to showcase their talents and to make their mark. In the decades that have followed that inaugural gathering in the 'Eternal City' – which was attended by 400 athletes from a total of 23 countries – the Games have witnessed many memorable moments, significant landmarks and feats of individual and collective brilliance. Today, more than half a century on, the record books still bear testament to many of those achievements.

Athletes parade at the
Opening Ceremony
of the Beijing 2008
Paralympic Games.

Paralympic Games records

The 52-year history of the Paralympic Games has seen plenty of remarkable sporting achievements, with an array of facts, figures and records providing the story behind every gold, silver and bronze. Here we pick out some of the best.

All-time medal table (top 30)

Country	Gold	Silver	Bronze	Total
USA	701	627	641	1969
Great Britain	527	503	492	1522
Canada	378	302	317	997
France	330	323	311	964
Australia	314	340	306	960
West Germany	300	253	230	783
Poland	241	228	187	656
Netherlands	250	216	184	650
Germany	170	209	213	592
Sweden	218	208	156	582
Spain	191	189	197	577
China	231	187	134	552
Italy	134	151	178	463
Israel	122	120	122	364
Austria	106	116	118	340
Japan	109	110	117	337
Norway	107	102	88	297
Denmark	97	88	102	287
South Korea	110	86	83	279
Switzerland	81	89	94	264
Finland	70	94	100	264
Mexico	87	84	81	252
South Africa	102	76	73	251
Belgium	77	84	76	237
Ireland	54	59	85	198
Brazil	42	69	66	187
Ukraine	52	54	67	173
Russia	55	49	62	166
New Zealand	59	45	48	152
Egypt	42	54	54	150

Original Paralympic Games sports
(Appeared at Rome 1960 Games)

Snooker	Basketball
Wheelchair Fencing	Swimming
Javelin	Table Tennis
Precision Javelin	Archery
Shot Put	Dartchery
Indian Club Throw	Pentathlon

Table Tennis was among the original Paralympic Games sports.

Newest sports

Rowing	Beijing 2008
Football 5-a-side	Athens 2004
Sailing	Sydney 2000
Wheelchair Rugby	Sydney 2000
Equestrian	Atlanta 1996
Wheelchair Tennis	Seoul 1988

Leading medal winners

Name	Country	Sport	G	S	B	Total	Games
Trischa Zorn	USA	Swimming	32	9	5	46	Arnhem 1980–Athens 2004
Roberto Marson	Italy	Wheelchair Fencing	16	7	3	26	Tokyo 1964–Toronto 1976
Jonas Jacobsson	Sweden	Shooting	16	1	8	25	Arnhem 1980–Beijing 2008
Claudia Hengst	W.Germany/ Germany	Swimming	13	4	8	25	Seoul 1988–Athens 2004
Heinz Frei	Switzerland	Athletics, Cycling	13	6	5	24	Stoke Mandeville/New York 1984–Beijing 2008
Siegmar Henker	W.Germany/ Germany	Archery, Athletics, Shooting, Swimming	12	9	2	23	Toronto 1976–Atlanta 1996
Franz Nietlispach	Switzerland	Athletics, Cycling	14	6	2	22	Toronto 1976–Beijing 2008
Junichi Kawai	Japan	Swimming	5	9	7	21	Barcelona 1992–Beijing 2008
Timothy McIsaac	Canada	Swimming	11	6	4	21	Toronto 1976–Seoul 1988
Noel Pedersen	Norway	Swimming	9	9	3	21	Seoul 1988–Sydney 2000
Chantal Petitclerc	Canada	Athletics	14	5	2	21	Barcelona 1992–Beijing 2008
Zipora Rubin-Rosenbaum	Israel	Athletics, Swimming, Table Tennis	11	4	6	21	Tokyo 1964–Seoul 1988
Rosaleen Gallagher	Ireland	Archery, Athletics, Swimming, Table Tennis	4	6	11	21	Tel Aviv 1968–Seoul 1988

Highest athlete participation

4,011	Beijing 2008
3,881	Sydney 2000
3,808	Athens 2004
3,259	Atlanta 1996
3,059	Seoul 1988
3,001	Barcelona 1992
2,090	Stoke Mandeville/ New York 1984
1,651	Arnhem 1980
1,288	Toronto 1976
926	Heidelberg 1972
782	Tel Aviv 1968
239	Rome 1960
138	Tokyo 1964

A record 3,951 athletes competed at the Beijing 2008 Paralympic Games.

Competing countries

Beijing 2008	**146**
Athens 2004	**135**
Sydney 2000	**122**
Atlanta 1996	**104**
Barcelona 1992	**83**
Seoul 1988	**60**
Stoke Mandeville/ New York 1984	**54**
Arnhem 1980	**42**
Toronto 1976	**40**
Heidelberg 1972	**41**
Tel Aviv 1968	**28**
Tokyo 1964	**19**
Rome 1960	**17**

Sydney 2000 was the first Paralympic Games staged in the Southern Hemisphere.

Host cities

1960	Rome, Italy	1988	Seoul, South Korea
1964	Tokyo, Japan	1992	Barcelona, Spain
1968	Tel Aviv, Israel	1996	Atlanta, USA
1972	Heidelberg, Germany	2000	Sydney, Australia
1976	Toronto, Canada	2004	Athens, Greece
1980	Arnhem, Netherlands	2008	Beijing, China
1984	Stoke Mandeville, GB/ New York, USA	2012	London, Great Britain

Paralympic Games landmarks

• **Rome 1960**	First officially recognised Games
• **Heidelberg 1972**	First quadriplegic events added. Demonstration events for athletes with visual impairment
• **Toronto 1976**	First use of specialised racing wheelchairs
• **Arnhem 1980**	Events for cerebral palsy athletes included
• **Seoul 1988**	Co-operation between Olympic and Paralympic Organising Committees
• **Atlanta 1996**	First worldwide corporate sponsorship of Games
• **Athens 2004**	Record media attendance for a Games

Specialised racing wheelchairs were first used at Toronto 1976.

Jessica Long won two individual Swimming gold medals at Athens 2004.

Youngest and oldest athletes

- **Oldest athlete at Beijing 2008:** 69-year-old Emilie Gradisek was part of the Slovenian Sitting Volleyball team

- **Youngest athlete at Beijing 2008:** Czech Katerina Komarkova (13) made her Paralympic Games debut in the Swimming events

- American swimmer **Jessica Long** was 12 years old when she won gold in the 100m Freestyle – S8 and 400m Freestyle – S8 at Athens 2004, making her the youngest-ever individual gold medallist at a Paralympic Games

Natalia Partyka (above) has played Table Tennis at three Paralympic Games and the Beijing 2008 Olympic Games while American Marla Runyan (right) competed in the Athletics programme in the Paralympic Games in 1992 and 1996 and the Olympic Games in 2000 and 2004.

Athletes competing in Paralympic Games and Olympic Games

- **Neroli Fairhall (New Zealand) – Archery**
  Competed at the Arnhem 1980 Paralympic Games and the Los Angeles 1984 Olympic Games

- **Paola Fantato (Italy) – Archery**
  Competed at five Paralympic Games (Seoul 1988–Athens 2004) and at the Atlanta 1996 Olympic Games

- **Marla Runyan (USA) – Athletics**
  Competed at two Paralympic Games (Barcelona 1992 and Atlanta 1996) and two Olympic Games (Sydney 2000 and Athens 2004)

- **Natalia Partyka (Poland) – Table Tennis**
  Competed at three Paralympic Games (Sydney 2000–Beijing 2008) and at the Beijing 2008 Olympic Games

- **Natalie du Toit (South Africa) – Swimming**
  Competed at two Paralympic Games (Athens 2004 and Beijing 2008) and at the Beijing 2008 Olympic Games

Paralympic Games factfile

- Apart from Rowing, which made its debut at Beijing 2008, Football 5-a-side is the only Paralympic Games sport that has always had the same champion: Brazil, who won gold at Athens 2004 and Beijing 2008

- There will be six different categories of disabilities competing at London 2012 (amputee, cerebral palsy, intellectually impaired, wheelchair, visually impaired and Les Autres). Only athletes with spinal cord injuries using wheelchairs participated at the inaugural Paralympic Games in Rome in 1960

- The worldwide television audience watching the Beijing 2008 Games was calculated at 3.8 billion total viewers – more than twice as many as the previous Games at Athens 2004

- The sports of Paralympic Canoeing and Paralympic Triathlon will be added to the competition programme at Rio 2016

The medals on offer at the London 2012
Paralympic Games – gold (centre), silver (left)
and bronze.

Picture credits

All images copyright Press Association Images
Except for the following: p16, p17 top, p18 bottom, p19 left, p19 bottom,
p20 top right, p21 bottom (© ODA); p19 top (Image by Populous)

Acknowledgements

Press Association Sport is a division of The Press Association, the national news
agency of the UK and Ireland, which was founded in 1868.

Head of Content: Peter Marshall
Chief Writer: Alex Brooker
Writer: Jon Mattos
Design: Mark Tattersall
Editor: Pete Thompson
Contributors: Frank Malley, Matthew Sherry, Mark Staniforth,
Andrew McDermott